Lacan
and
Theological
Discourse

SUNY Series in Philosophy
Robert Cummings Neville, Editor

Lacan
and
Theological
Discourse

Edited by

Edith Wyschogrod
David Crownfield
Carl A. Raschke

With an Introduction by David H. Fisher
and Comments by David Crownfield

State University of New York Press

Published by
State University of New York Press, Albany

©1989 State University of New York

For information, address State University of New York
Press, State University Plaza, Albany, NY 12246

Library of Congress Cataloging-in-Publication Data

Lacan and theological discourse/edited by Edith Wyschogrod, David
  Crownfield, Carl A. Raschke; with an introduction by David H.
  Fisher and comments by David Crownfield.
      p.   cm. – (SUNY series in philosophy)
  Bibliography: p.
  Includes index.
  ISBN 0-7914-0110-3.   – ISBN 0-7914-0111-1 (pbk.)
    1. Psychoanalysis and religion.   2. Lacan, Jacques, 1901-
  3. Languages – Religious aspects.   I. Wyschogrod, Edith.
  II. Crownfield, David, 1930-   III. Raschke, Carl A.   IV. Series.
  BF175.4.R44L33   1989
  230'.092'4 – dc19   88-37648
                                                                          CIP

        63,807

  10 9 8 7 6 5 4 3 2 1

Contents

Acknowledgments

"The Pathology of the Father's Rule: Lacan and the Symbolic," by Charles E. Scott. Originally published in *Thought*, 61 (March, 1986), 119-130. Used by permission of the publisher.

"God and the Utopianism of Language," by Gabriel Vahanian in *God and Language*, eds. Robert Scharlemann and Gilbert M. Ogutu (New York: Paragon House, 1987), 194-206. Originally prepared for a conference arranged by the New Ecumenical Research Association; held in Seoul, Korea, August, 1984. Used by permission of the publisher.

The editors wish to thank Marilyn Semerad for the unusual care she showed in producing this volume.

Re-Marks

Does Jacques Lacan have anything to say to theology? Or, to restate the question in Lacan-like terms, can his remarks re-mark the texts and themes of religion so that through them the unconscious speaks? This question takes in the blind unconsciousness of the theologian's own desires (the psychological issue); the margins, blanks, or spaces of religious texts that address her or him (the hermeneutical issue); the hidden desires that lurk in sacramental rites (the sociopolitical issue). But the truly bold dimension of this question is the encounter it provokes with *God's* desire. The divine eros must be brought into the daylight of language. Truly this is what has been called the double genitive with a vengeance: the desire of God means the theologian's desire *for* God as well as the desire belonging *to* God. But what could God desire? Another? Is God not then complete? But if another, what other? That which is other than God, an abyss or nothingness other than the wholly Other?

Lacan rarely addresses theological problems head on. Still, Augustine was a favorite text he never ceased to ponder, for its obsession with lack and love, with memory and language, is his own. And on the rare occasions when he addresses texts, often the most well-trodden of these, he does so with a reverent irreverence; reverent because he knows that great texts contain a refractory and secret "more," and irreverent because he shamelessly trespasses on the hidden. Thus he does not hesitate to examine (after Kierkegaard) the biblical account of the sacrifice of Isaac. It is the master text (if such a notion were tolerable to Lacan) for understanding the role of the father in bringing the child into culture and making him a member of society. In the biblical text, Lacan tells us, God as El Shadday is "he who chooses, he who promises, who causes a certain covenant—which is transmissible in only one way, through the paternal *barachah* [blessing]—to pass through his name."[1] Lacan avers that the ninth-century rabbinic commentator, Rashi, breaches the abyss of the text when he (Rashi) declares that the angel reveals to Abraham that Abraham has not come to the mountain to sacrifice Isaac but for a deeper reason. Uncomprehending, Abraham responds that if he has not come for nothing, he must at least inflict a slight wound on Isaac. With Rashi's help, Lacan claims he has penetrated the secret of the text as understood by the Mishnah (the traditional second-century Jewish compilation of formulaic commentaries on Biblical verses). "[T]he ram in question is the primeval ram" from which one can infer that it was there during the seven days of the creation.[2] From this Lacan boldly concludes the sacrificial ram is one of the *Elohim* or local gods, the very deity who is Abraham's own eponymous ancestor. More daring still, Lacan claims: "Here may be marked the knife blade separating God's bliss from what in that tradition is presented as his desire."[3] Lacan must be read as focusing just here because only here does the blade of the knife cut off desire so that an inundation of desires is forestalled. The sexual rites of communion with God are marked off, that is to say re-marked, so that, unlike Canaanite desire, Israelite desire will encounter over and over again covenant and command, Torah, the Law of the Father.

However insightful or shocking—Lacan's desire to wound and astound are well known—Lacan's impact cannot be traced to his own efforts at glossing traditional texts, or to interpreting theological problematics. It is rather to Lacan's break with standard discourse that theologians turn to see what there is in Lacan's treatment of desire, absence, and lack, of the Other and most particularly of the reading of psychological life in terms of its linguistic character, that interests and provokes. No longer can psychoanalysis merely declare God a projection in order reductively to dismiss the necessity of further interpretation. Instead the open-ended inquiry into the unconscious dimensions of the sacred and of the self offers itself as an infinite theological task. The theologian, in this sense like the psychoanalyst, stands before the bubbling up of desire and its transposition into language. She or he is like Lacan's prefeminist woman who "prepares herself on the off-chance . . . that her inner fantasy of Man [L'homme] will find its hour of truth."[4] But if the theologian imagines truth as a resting place, Lacan concludes the previous remark about truth with the daring and feminist re-mark, "[T]ruth is already woman insofar as it's not-all, unable, in any case to be wholly-spoken."[5]

The impetus for the present collection arose at a plenary session on Lacan at the American Academy of Religion meeting in Atlanta in 1986. The fervor of both the enthusiasm and criticism that this packed session generated suggested to some of its participants that many more persons with an interest in recent theology, postmodern philosophy, and literary criticism, as well as in recent developments in psychoanalytic theory, might wish to see these as well as other re-marks about

Lacan's importance for the philosophy and psychology of religion in a single volume. With this thought in mind, the editors gathered several essays into a collection whose first version (Winquist and Wyschogrod) was launched at the Academy's meeting, and solicited further work from those who have been in theological and philosophical conversation with Lacan (Earle, Raschke, Taylor, Scott, and Vahanian). For those who wonder how this enterprise meshes with other interdisciplinary uses of Lacan, as well as how he fits on the map of recent psychoanalytic work, David H. Fisher has written an introduction in non-Lacanian language. David Crownfield, a coeditor of this collection, has appended his comments after each article. These re-mark the strands of the argument and critically engage each contributor's text. On Lacan's reading, no text is successful, that is, tells the truth. The editors have no desire to transcend this claim. Could Lacan's view of this project be made known, he might reissue a comment made in another connection, that "truth is more often than not standoffish . . . misfiring sure as clockwork."

Edith Wyschogrod

Notes

1. Jacques Lacan, "Introduction to the Names-of-the-Father Seminar," in *October*, 40 (Spring, 1987): 92.

2. Ibid., 92.

3. Ibid.

4. Jacques Lacan, "Television," in *October*, 40 (Spring, 1987): 92.

5. Ibid., 44 f.

Introduction

Framing Lacan?

David H. Fisher

> Lacan speaks about everything under the sun and calls it psychoanal-
> ysis. How can we frame him? Especially since he ... fundamentally
> challenges the notion of the frame: in his Seminar of 11 May 1976 he
> tells the story of James Joyce, who one day is asked a question about
> an image which reproduces an aspect of the city of Cork. Joyce replies
> that it is Cork. The fellow says, I recognize it, but what is framing it?
> To which Joyce replies: 'Cork'[liege].
> —Juliet Flower MacCannell, *Figuring Lacan*

The current volume of essays explores some major issues for the relationship between religion and contemporary culture raised by the work
of a French psychoanalyst, philosopher, and critic of culture, Jacques
Lacan (1901-1981). My objective is not to introduce the essayists; this
will be undertaken in comments following each section. It is, despite
his resistance to framing, to introduce — to frame — Lacan.

The frame intended here is a limited one. The importance of
Lacan's work is highlighted for the reader by calling attention to some
representative examples of the scope of his influence. In order to grasp
the radical character of Lacan's thought, I shall first consider his potential contribution to the growing "culture of psychology" debate among
sociologists and cultural critics concerned with the impact of psychoanalytic practice and theory on contemporary Western culture.

Attention is then devoted to four main concepts. The first is Lacan's
contribution to psychoanalytic theory and practice, as it bears on various post-Freudian revisions of Freud's several models of the mind and,
more specifically, on Freud's understanding of the nature and function
of the ego in psychoanalysis. The second topic is Lacan's contribution
to the debate, within and outside of psychoanalysis, about the proper
context for reading Freud. At stake is the difference between those

1

who advocate interpreting Freud in the context of modern science and those who place Freud within the context of modern (and post-modern) hermeneutics. The third area to be explored is Lacan's contribution to discussions among linguists and literary and film critics about the nature of language and its role in the formation of the subject. Finally, there is Lacan's potential contribution to the dialogue between religion and psychoanalysis. Many of the essayists represented here have been involved in the critical and constructive development of post-modern forms of theology (or a/theology), and have thus responded to Lacan from philosophical and theological perspectives on cultural issues. But there is also an extensive body of scholarship on the relationship between religion and psychoanalysis with roots in the clinical practice of therapy. To see the difference between an earlier-view relationship of theology and psychoanalysis and the radically new perspectives offered here, I shall contrast the philosophical/theological/ cultural foci of this volume with more clinically based perspectives represented by that other body of scholarship.

Dimensions of Cultural Influence: Lacan and the "Culture of Psychology"

The broad influence of Jacques Lacan's work is evident in a number of areas of contemporary culture. A recent bibliography[1] on Lacan lists no less than forty-eight books that are either about Lacan or are devoted to major aspects of his work in English, one hundred and twenty-one articles, and four other bibliographies! *Dissertation Abstracts* reveals more than one hundred dissertations over the past ten years in which Lacan or his ideas play an important role, ranging across a variety of fields: film criticism, philosophy, psychology, and literary criticism, to name only the major categories.

The emergence of this "Lacan industry" in English is but one example of the broader impact of contemporary continental thought in a variety of disciplines on intellectual life in America and Great Britain. If one believes that it is important to come to terms with structural, post-structural, or deconstructive thought, a knowledge of Lacan and his work is inescapable from the perspective of his current influence, if nothing else. Juliet MacCannell notes that "every major figure in French intellectual life of the last 30 years was touched by him in important ways: Barthes, Foucault, Kristeva, Sollers, Althusser, Mannoni, Ricoeur, Derrida et al. attended his seminars; his close friends included surrealist poets . . . and the great Structuralists, Levi-Strauss, Jakobson, and Benveniste."[2]

While this wider dimension of Lacanian influence is both complex and important, in a different sense Lacan's cultural impact can be understood as a countervailing force to literature, primarily identified with American sociological studies of psychology in terms of their impact on contemporary American life. This "culture," as understood by authors such as Philip Rieff[3], Jules Henry[4], Christopher Lasch[5], Richard Sennett[6] and Peter Homans[7], is depicted in varying ways.

Homans, for example, in his discussion of the theory of "mass society" or "massification" as a "total outlook," has explored the ways in which the psychoanalytic tradition has influenced social and cultural life. The cultural crisis of Western man is interpreted in terms of a lack of contact with a viable tradition, a sense of depersonalization and loss of autonomy, and as relating to social order either in patterns of alienation or of submissive conformity. These phenomenona are then used to account for major issues in modern politics, culture, and community life[8].

While Homans tends to be neutral in his evaluation of the impact of psychoanalysis on culture, Rieff, Sennett, and Lasch have, in different ways, depicted psychoanalysis as a contributing factor to the withdrawal of many persons (especially members of the "culture elite") from a sustained concern for the common good and public life, in what is characterized by Lasch at least as a "culture of narcissism." The "psychoanalytic attitude" is said to foster an amoral or "remissive" culture, in which the need to accept moral responsibility for social conditions is replaced with a therapeutic dissolution of feelings of guilt. Psychoanalysis, it is argued, encourages a preoccupation with one's inner life at the expense of public concerns. In Robert N. Bellah's book, *Habits of the Heart*[9], Bellah and his colleagues reemphasize this general picture of the negative impact of therapy on cultural life, although there has been notable dissent from that picture.[10]

Whereas most of this literature on the "culture of psychology" has adopted a sociological approach to the impact of psychoanalysis on American cultural life, Lacan with his repeated denunciations of what he sees as the misdirection of American ego psychology, offers another and quite different perspective. Lacan's position, although not incompatible with current clinical interest among American psychoanalysts in the characterization of "narcissistic disorders" by Otto Kernberg or Heinz Kohut, understands the etiology of such disorders differently.

Lacan's major contribution to this discussion of the culture of psychoanalysis lies in his radical relocation of fundamental human problems which are, for him, rooted in an analysis of desire. For Lacan, "desire discovers its signification in the desire of the Other . . . because the real object of desire is to be recognized and desirable.[11]. This approach opens the way toward what Norman Holland has called

"postmodern psychoanalysis," in which emphasis is placed on the intersubjective identity created in the psychoanalytic relationship and its
parallels to relationships between persons in society: "[Postmodern] psychoanalysis allows us to explore the space between ourselves and the
people and things around us, including other disciplines and sciences"[12].
A Lacanian emphasis on the dialectic of desire has intellectual roots in
Hegel, transmitted to Lacan through Alexander Kojève's Marxist
reading,[13] and offers an alternative way of conceptualizing the culture
of psychoanalysis.

"Desire," in Lacan, emerges from an inexpressible lack, a void
associated with Freud's death instinct:

> The death instinct is that radical force which surfaces in the cata-
> strophic or ecstatic instant when the organic coherence of the body
> appears as though unnamed and unnameable, a swoon or ecstasy,
> screaming out its appeal for a word to veil or sustain it. It constitutes
> the basis of the castration complex and allows the development of
> language, together with the possibility of desire and the development
> of the sexual instincts.[14]

Desire develops from a fundamental rupture or split early in the life
of each human subject. This split is initially *represented* (in very early
human development) in (imaginary) images of a fragmentary, split self,
contrasted with an image of being whole, satisfied, or unified, in a
"mirror image." The impossibility of unifying the subject's fragmentary
experience of himself with the assimilated whole images produced by
the desire of another human "subject of desire" creates this split. These
inchoate images are radically transformed—made human, as Lacan
argues—when the child is "born into language." Desire in its specifically human sense emerges when the subject finds himself as a want-
to-be within the rules and conventions of language and society. This is
Lacan's "Symbolic order," presided over by the "Name of the Father."
Lacan asserts.

> The moment in which desire becomes human is also that in which
> the child is born into language. The subject is not simply mastering
> his privation by assuming it, but ... is raising his desire to a second
> power, for his action destroys the subject that it [the action] causes to
> appear and disappear in the anticipating provocation of its absence
> and presence. His action thus negatives the field of force of desire in
> order to become its own object to itself ... the desire of the child has
> become the desire of another, of an *alter ego* ... whose object of desire
> is henceforth his own affliction. So when we wish to attain in the

subject what was before the serial articulations of speech, and what is primordial to the birth of symbols, we find it in death.[15]

By pointing to a fundamental fragmentation or split within the subject that cannot be healed or made whole, whether by therapy or by the incorporation of inherited cultural-value traditions, Lacan is criticizing the critique of the "culture of narcissism." To the extent that modern culture is founded on the Cartesian notion of a unified subject, certain of his origins, or on an understanding of individual existence over against culture, it is founded, for Lacan, on an error. Psychoanalysis, properly understood, is neither a technique to help individuals adapt to the pressures of an alienating, dehumanizing "mass" culture (through the maintenance of a strong ego), nor is it, as the critical literature avers, an excuse for preoccupation with the narcissistic self at the expense of society. It is, in fact, a critical hermeneutic of both self and culture based on a fundamental insight into the role of language in the formation of the self. But to grasp Lacan's importance for a revision of this widely used notion of a "culture of psychoanalysis," it is necessary to turn one's attention toward Lacan's role in debates within the subculture of the theory and practice of psychoanalysis itself.

Lacan's Critique of the Ego in Psychoanalytic Theory and Practice

Lacan's importance is pivotal in the current debates within the theory and practice of psychoanalysis about its grounding and future directions. This debate includes such issues as the centrality of the ego in models of the mind and the question of adaptation to one's culture as a proper goal of clinical practice. In the context of the American psychoanalytic scene, Lacan's influence is felt at the level of both metapsychology and clinical practice.

Two major revisions of Freudian theory, object-relations theory and self-psychology, have had a strong influence on contemporary American discussions of the foundations for psychoanalysis. Freud devoted most of his work to a discussion of the origins of neuroses in the Oedipal complex, whereas these neo-Freudian theories of human development investigate the roots of trauma occurring at a pre-Oedipal stage (or stages) of development.

These different understandings of pre-Oedipal human stages of develpment vary considerably. In her discussion of psychoanalytically influenced theories of the earliest stages of human development, Victoria Hamilton suggests that Freud and varying post-Freudian theories (such as those of Mahler, Kohut, Klein, Kernberg, Rosenfeld, Bowlby, Bower, Brazelton, and Winicott) can be arranged on a spectrum.

Descriptions of the primary undifferentiated fusion between mother
and infant range from "passive or negative orientations" toward the
first stages of life (fusion, unity, bliss, autism, psychosis, chaos, terror)
to "active and positive orientations," in which the infant is understood not only to be more active, but also "more connected to, sen-
sorially aware of, and positively oriented toward, his primary attachment figure."[16]

Self-psychology and object-relations theory have developed understandings of self-formation and of the purposes of analysis which share
the common legacy of American ego psychology, most clearly seen in
the work of Heinz Hartmann,[17] and his subsequent influence on American psychoanalytic theory and practice. Both address the now wide-
spread phenomena of narcissistic character disorders — grandiosity,
idealization, splitting — as manifestations of a disorder which requires
curative treatment. The difference is that where Kernberg and object-
relations theory generally view such phenomena as defenses against early
massive feelings of love and hate, to be dissolved by analytic insight,
Kohut and self-psychology view them as manifestations of an early defect
in self-development which require empathic support to be mended.

Lacan, by contrast, has consistently attacked the ideal of ego
strengthening and adaptation to one's culture as appropriate goals of
psychoanalysis, and has argued for a return to what he believes to be
one of Freud's major but neglected insights: that the ego is essentially a
defense formation, not a nucleus around which a self can be built, and
that there is no such thing as a "total person" or "total self"; the subject, as already noted, originates in the split between a disjunctive and
a unified image of itself. This unified image is given to the infant,
either through a literal seeing of its mirror image, or through the infant's
internalization of its coherent image in the "gaze of the Other," and the
ego is then formed around it. The unified image is not the subject's
experience of itself, but its experience of self *as seen from the outside*.
The subject is split between an unconscious desire and the ego that
protects the subject from that desire.

In clinical practice, Lacan is known for his innovations — the variable time of analytic sessions being the most famous or infamous. His
followers in this country have begun to make their weight felt in debates
over the proper goals of analytic training as well as of clinical practice.
For example, growing interest in parallels between the work of psychoanalysis and literary criticism is evident in Roy Schaefer's influential
discussion of psychoanalytic dialogue as a narrative:

> One might say that, in the course of analysis there develops a cluster
> of more or less coordinated new narrations, each corresponding to

periods of intense analytic work on certain leading questions . . . The psychoanalytic dialogue is characterized most of all by its organization in terms of the here and now of the psychoanalytic relationship. It is fundamentally a dialogue concerning the present moment of transference and resistance . . . It is a story that begins in the middle, which is the present: the beginning is the beginning of analysis.[18]

Schaefer's position can be compared with three Lacanian propositions about narrative:

(1) Narration is structured like a (subject in) language; (2) narration's manifest content is a product of the unconscious discourse that is both the precondition of narration and the site of its appearances (so that the subject of narration . . . will always be other than what is signified in narration); (3) the unconscious discourse of language and its processes are revealed in the "gaps" or "lapses" that appear in a narrative's manifest text (narrative interpretation . . . [is] a contingent effect within the larger unconscious discourse of the Other).

Lacan understands literature and psychoanalysis as forms of critique of an egocentric, androcentric point of view, and uses structural or poststructural technique in his narrative analysis. Both the linguistic strategy employed and the social-political struggle against what Lacan perceived as the ideologization of psychoanalysis proceed from a different set of cognitive and cultural assumptions than Schaefer's more classical models of narrative and his views on the goals of psychoanalysis.

Another way to observe the clinical distinction between other neo-Freudian approaches such as Kohut's, and Lacan's call for a "return to Freud," is to contrast their respective understandings of cure. Kohut claims that "psychoanalysis cures by the laying down of psychological structure."[20] Kohut works from an optimal picture of the unified human self:

Throughout his life a person will experience himself as a cohesive harmonious firm unit in time and space, connected with his past and pointing meaningfully into a creative-productive future, but only as long as, at each stage in his life, he experiences certain representatives of his human surroundings as joyfully responding to him, as available to him as sources of idealized strength and calmness, as being silently present but in essence like him.[21]

Based on this image of human personality and development, Kohut claims that the proper psychoanalytic response to fragmentation or defects in the self is one which enables the analysand to overcome or repair fragmentation. This was to be accomplished by first reactivating the defects (or their approximate causes) during the analytic session, and then responding to them with a behavioral analogy (on the part of the analyst) to the missing, adequate "self-object" function depicted above—serving as a source of strength, calmness, and so on. Kohut describes this process as a sequence in which there is "reactivation of need . . . non-response by the self-object [analyst] . . . [and] re-establishment of a bond of empathy between self and self-object . . ."[22] The emphasis here—on mending repair, and the goals of a coherent self with firm boundaries—employs a different model of the mind from that of earlier American ego psychology. Although self is the preferred Kohutian term for the whole person, in distinction to the ego as a part of the mental apparatus, there is still an obvious family resemblance in the common concern of both perspectives for the adaptation and unification of the subject.

Lacanian psychoanalysis, by contrast, holds that Freud did not provide a term for the total person in his metapsychology because he was convinced that there was no such thing as a total person or total self.[23] As a result, the Lacanian notion of cure is different from Freud's: there will always be a fundamental division within the subject. A major task of psychoanalysis is to enable a recognition by the divided subject of that truth.

> The distinction between the true subject of desire—the "I"—and the ego—that which conceals the"I"—is crucial to the psychoanalytic enterprise. The object, then, of psychoanalysis is the recognition by the analysand of himself as a true subjectivity who, in effect, orders his own experience of reality and no longer as a victim of objectifications which . . . is the personification of his own ego. The ultimate termination of analysis is made when the patient discovers that only he himself—and not his ego—possesses his own truth.[24]

This concern for the truth of the subject, as opposed to an illusory identification of the subject with the ego, links Lacan to Freud's own insistence on truth over illusion—and is also, as subsequent discussion will show, a major basis for Derrida's rejection of Lacan's position.

These differences between Lacan and American psychoanalysis—in both their understanding of models of the mind and of the methods and goals of clinical practice—can also be viewed as aspects of a broader controversy to which Lacan and Lacanians have made important contributions, namely, the proper context for a construal of the nature of psychoanalysis as a practice, and for the work of Freud as the founder of psychoanalysis. Where representatives of the mainstream tradition of American psychoanalysis have tended – in varying degrees and in varying contexts of debate and discussion – to insist on both the medical model and the natural scientific character of psychoanalysis, the perspective initiated by Lacan has understood psychoanalysis as a linguistic science devoted to the study of the speech which takes place during the analytic encounter.

Psychoanalysis: Natural Science or Hermeneutic of Desire?

Jeffery Mehlman, a leading exponent of psychoanalytic readings of texts, notes that "if one were to isolate the distinctive trait characterizing a number of recent French readings of Freud, it would perhaps be the effort to read Freud's theoretical texts with the attention to surprising repetitions and displacements of meaning normally brought to bear on clinical data."[25] Lacan's reading of Freud is a major if not the major source for this approach to Freud's texts. Where most Lacanians seem interested in a dialogue with alternative hermeneutic readings, such as those of Paul Ricoeur, it is useful here to consider a position which rejects the hermeneutic interpretation of Freud altogether.

The Foundations of Psychoanalysis: A Philosophical Critique, by Adolf Grunbaum,[26] on the one hand challenges the validity of any hermeneutic approach to Freud's work, as represented by both Jurgen Habermas and Paul Ricoeur; and on the other it attacks the problematic status of psychoanalysis as science from the perspective of the philosophy of science. On the first point, Grunbaum ignores the ambiguities of meaning in Freud's language. No attention is given to linkages between Freud's work and literature, such as the parallels, noted by critics like Lionel Trilling as well as by Lacan, between Freud's mechanisms of displacement and condensation in dream work, and the operation of the tropes of metaphor, metonymy, and synecdoche. Nor is attention given to the Romantic as well as anti-Romantic and Enlightenment motifs in Freud's thought, much less to the fact that Freud's one major award during his lifetime was the Goethe prize – for literature.

On the second point, Grunbaum neglects Lacan's suggestion that the proper model for scientific theory applicable to psychoanalysis is to be found in linguistics. Instead, Grunbaum insists on the absolute separation between science and nonscience. Lacan and those who follow him question this dichotomy, understanding psychoanalysis as a science shaped by its object, the analysis of speech. Grunbaum's work assumes that

> Freud forsook his initial, ontological reductive notion of scientific status in favor of a methodological, epistemic one .... [W]hen Freud

unswervingly claimed natural science status for his theoretical constructions throughout his life, he did so first and foremost for his
evolving clinical theory of personality and therapy, rather than for
the metapsychology . . . . [H]e perennially saw himself entitled to proclaim scientificity [*sic.*] of his clinical theory to proclaim strength of a
secure and direct epistemic warrant from the observations he made
of his patients and of himself.[27]

Grunbaum's conclusions, based on citations from Freud's work that
are sometimes taken out of context misses a major point of Freud's
discovery from a Lacanian perspective: that *all* discourse (including
the writing of the founder of psychoanalysis) is overdetermined. Cognition is governed by narcissism and desire, so that the analyst's desire
can no more be overlooked or avoided than the desire of the analysand. This means that one must attend to the unconscious linguistic
structure of theoretical and metatheoretical discourse, as well as to
that of analysands, in order to grasp the forces at work determining
the production of such texts. There is no such thing as "pure" or "literal" speech.

To be sure, not all hermeneutic readings of Freud agree with either
the strategy or conclusions pursued by Lacan. As William Kerrigan has
noted, Paul Ricoeur presupposes Lacan from the beginning to the end
of his major work on philosophy and psychoanalysis, *Freud and Philosophy,* but interprets the underpinnings of psychoanalysis in a different
way. Ricoeur defends Freud's notion of psychic energy as a concept
poised between biology and semantics, reducible to neither, and then
argues that Lacan's linguistic unconscious can be discarded as an unten-
able distortion.[28] Nevertheless, Ricoeur agrees with Lacan on the importance of attending to Freud from a hermeneutic rather than a natural
scientific perspective.

Obviously, the question of how Freud is to be read is more complex than these brief, comparative remarks have suggested. The inten-
sity of the debate between those determined to place Freud primarily
within clinical practice, the history of (natural) science, or the (linguistic/
symbolic) hermeneutic of culture is further complicated by those determined to dismiss Freud and his work altogether. Critics reject Freud's
"outmoded ideas" in contrast to recent neurobiological and sociogenetic
research. Others, like Grunbaum, note a poor evidential basis for his
theories, or inadequate theory construction, while others, writing from
various radical perspectives, see Freud as the prisoner of culturally
conditioned Victorian repressions or of a male-dominated society. What
Lacan offers to those concerned with such matters is a radically different placement of Freud's achievement.

Lacan On Language: Structural or Post-Structural?

Lacan's reading of Freud and his clinical practice clearly show the influence of structural theories of language. Two major questions for Lacan scholarship concern the nature and extent of that influence and whether — or to what degree — Lacan's texts are to be seen as "structural" or as "poststructural". To deal with both issues requires a context provided by modern philosophical influence on linguistic theory.

Contemporary analyses of language in general, and discussions of the relationship between meaning and reference in particular, share a common point of departure in Kant, who sought to find a balance between the metaphysical certainty of continental rationalism and British epistemological skepticism through his transcendental analysis of the structures of cognition. Kant's solution posited universal epistemic structures of the knowing subject which were assumed to be themselves knowable, even though the relationship of such structures to either extra subjective reality or to the subject as a substratum of knowing remained in doubt. The Kantian legacy was subsequently challenged by questions concerning the possibility of establishing even the transcendental structures of knowledge. Discussions of such challenges usually include consideration of Marx's insistence on the formative role of ideological perspectives on consciousness; Freud's claims about the ways in which the ego in its role as censor necessarily distorts perception in response to the demands of the unconscious; and Nietzsche's arguments about the figurative character of all language.

This philosophical movement away from questions of extra linguistic reference is continued in structuralism, as presented in the linguistic theories of Ferdinand de Saussure, and in the anthropological-sociological application of Saussure's work in Claude Levi-Strauss. The matter of extralinguistic reference is put aside — "bracketed" (as the noumenal world is "bracketed" in Husserlian phenomenology in favor of an eidetic analysis of the structure of appearances). Linguistics is understood as a science devoted to the study of signs, and each verbal sign is said to combine two elements, the *signifier* (the letters and words of written or spoken language) and the *signified* (the concepts or meanings which the signifiers represent). Meaning, in this perspective, is not a function of reference to an extralinguistic object, but of the difference between linguistic units or chains of signifiers, and is constituted by the difference between each unit or chain, that is, the phoneme is defined by its alternatives, the sign by its alternatives, and so on. This does not mean that structuralism explicitly denies that a world may exist independently of language, but simply that it denies that there is any way in which human beings ever "get beyond" language to the "thing itself." Signifiers refer to signifieds—not to things. We are within what Frederick Jameson has called the "prisonhouse of language." In a larger cultural sense, this "linguistic paradigm" of human knowing extended beyond structuralism to dominate much contemporary discussion among linguists and literary and sociocultural theories affected by Continental thought.

In several respects, Lacan clearly shows the influence not only of Saussure and Levi Strauss but also of another prominent structural linguist, R. Jakobson. Muller and Richardson have shown, in *Lacan and Language*,[29] the impact of Saussure, from whom Lacan drew the notion of a split between signifier (the actual letters or sounds of language) and the signified (the concepts which the signifiers represent within the unity of a sign). Lacan also made use of Saussure's distinction between speech (*parole*) and language (*langue*). Speech, for both Saussure and Lacan, is the *diachronic* (spread out over time) flow of discourse, while language is the *synchronic* (seen all at once) structure governing possible patterns of linguistic meaning. Where Saussure hesitated to proclaim the impossibility of (extralinguistic) truth, Lacan went further. Truth, or "the Real" in Lacan's sense, is impossible because it is literally beyond all speech, beyond even the fluid, presymbolic structure of images which constitute imaginary ego-identifications. From Jakobson, Lacan gained the notion that all units of meaning could be understood along one of two fundamental axes of language: combination (metonymy, in the classic rhetorical theory of tropes), in which units are related by their sequential relationships; and selection or displacement (metaphor), in which meaning occurs by mutual exclusion.

But it was Levi-Strauss, an anthropologist, whose essays apparently had the strongest impact on Lacan. The notion that the unconscious consists of the aggregate of structural laws, by which individual experiences are transformed into living myth, seems to have led Lacan to think of the unconscious as "structured like a language." Further, Levi-Strauss's argument that sructural linguistics should be the paradigm for analysis in all social sciences in which the demands of a rigorous mathematical study are met is evident in Lacan's many references to psychoanalysis as a linguistic science, a science of the signifier. All of these borrowings locate Lacan within the sphere of structuralism.

However, Ellie Ragland-Sullivan argues that Lacan accepted Levi-Strauss's reversal of Saussure's signified-signifier relationship only to go beyond it.

> Although he accepted Levi-Strauss's reversal of the signifier and signified relationship [placing the signifier in the ascendant structuring position], Lacan's return to the idea that the 'sign' denotes language

in its concrete character marked his departure from anthropology . . .
Lacan's total enterprise undertook to show that unconscious language
is the language of indestructible Desire—a meaning chain of dead
signifiers. In this scheme the structuralist conception of language as
an instrument of word-transmission-message breaks down, because
the peculiar quality of Lacanian *parole* is to make heard what it does
not say . . . Lacan proposed the signified as unconscious meaning that
does not 'hear' or think itself.[30]

The apparent privileging of the signifier over the signified in Lacan
is just the point at which Jacques Derrida, writing from a deconstructive
perspective, challenges Lacan. From his earliest work to his most recent,
Derrida questions the "natural" primacy of speech over writing (in
Derrida's expanded sense of the word writing[31]), and, in protest, the
notion of being able to arrive at any single "Truth" including the truth
of the analyst. Although Lacan clearly made the Symbolic Order
(consisting of signifiers, symbols, and cultural meanings) the basis for
both psychoanalytic theory and practice, it is equally clear that Lacan
believes signifiers to have been built up (in ways determined by the
nature of language) out of a dialectic of signifieds (images) in the Imaginary order. In all of this, Derrida finds a lingering form of idealism, of
imperfectly digested or criticized Hegelianism. Further, he discovers in
Lacan a type of logocentricism as well, in which nostalgia for the logos,
presence, "full speech," leads one to believe that the "truth" of the
subject can be found by the analytical "lifting of the veil".

Having first raised these criticisms, along with some attacks on
Lacan's duplicity, in a preliminary way in a 1971 interview,[32] Derrida
has since continued his argument at greater length in "Le Facteur de la
Verité"[33] (a deconstructive reading of Lacan's famous seminar on Edgar
Allen Poe's "The Purloined Letter"), and in remarks made at the University of Montreal in 1979.[34] According to Derrida, the analyst is the
"maker of truth," in the sense that he alone separates the true from the
inauthentic "text" of the psychoanalytic dialogue:

> Henceforth, a text, if it is living and animated, full and authentic,
> will be of value only by virtue of the speech it will have as its mission
> to transport. Therefore, there will also be full texts and empty texts
> . . . One cannot define the 'hermeneutical circle,' along with all the
> conceptual parts of its system, more rigorously or more faithfully.[35]

Derrida's entire work has been focused on the continuation of
Heidegger's "destruction" of metaphysics, through a critical attack on
any "transcendental signified" that would guarantee the "identity"

or "truth" of a written text. Derrida has sought, instead, to demonstrate the intertextual deferral or indeterminacy of all textual meaning
through deconstructive analysis. It is hardly surprising, therefore, that
Derrida should interpret the psychoanalytic unveiling of Lacan's "Phallus" (the transcendental, abstract signifier of an impossible, unified
identity within the subject that cannot be "cut") as an appropriate
object for deconstructive attack. While both men clearly work out of
the legacy of Hegel, Lacan has taken Hegel's understanding of the dialectic of desire presented in the *Phenomenology* as his primary text, and
has then transposed it into Freud's discovery concerning the "Drives"
(*Trieb*). Derrida, on the other hand, is attempting to create a space for
philosophical thought in the light of Hegel's apparent claim (in pas-
sages from the *Encyclopedia Logic* and other late texts) to have brought
"closure" to philosophy; to have been the "last" philosopher who
brought together all history and all thought in a single, universal idealistic system in which the "Real is rational." Lacan, helped by Kojève's
Marxist reading of the *Phenomenology*, finds in the materiality of the
signifier and its relationship to desire, the basis for analysis. Derrida,
rejecting the limitations of Marx's criticism of Hegel, seeks to undermine all possible foundations, including those to be found in the unconscious dialectic of desire.

　　This debate occurs both at the level of Lacan's theory construction and at the level of Lacan's linguistic practice. The playful, allusive,
and elusive character of Lacan's style might seem to bring him closer to
post-structural practice, with its tendency to construct texts which defer,
resist, or avoid any single, unitary interpretation. Derrida suggests otherwise when he notes that he is "skipping over the rhetoric, Lacan's
style: its sometimes remarkable, and also sometimes anachronistic (I
do not say untimely) effects . . . seemed to me to be governed by the
delay of a scene, conferring upon it, as I do not doubt, a certain necessity. (I am designating whatever constrained him to deal with institu-
tionalized psychoanalysis in a certain way: this is Lacan's argument.)"[36]
What Derrida is suggesting is that Lacan's style is a tactic, designed to
undermine the French and international psychoanalytic establishment,
partly for political purposes, as well as to increase Lacan's authority
over his hearers, and not an attempt to echo the "discourse of the Other."

　　One must remember, in considering the question of Lacan's style,
the sociopolitical context of Lacan's work, as well as the psychoanalytic
framework of unmasking and attending within which he functions as
a therapist. If, as I have argued in the discussion of Lacan's contribution to debates within psychoanalysis, his primary objective at the level
of clinical practice is that of undermining the duplicity of the ego as a
defensive system, one might expect him to employ a style that would

evade the kind of control or lucid analysis adopted by the ego as a defense against the unconscious. It is not easy, given this practical context, to grasp the range of motivations which may have led to the style.

One way in which to answer the question of Lacan's structuralism or post-structuralism is to return to his most widely cited claim the "the unconscious is structured like a language." Within the field of psychoanalytic practice, this claim can be seen as a response to Freud's distinction between the "primary process" of the unconscious and the "secondary process" of consciousness, and his apparent desire to throw the critical light of conscious, "secondary process" thinking on the hidden depths of the id. "Where id was, there let ego be" is, for Lacan, an utter mistranslation of Freud's intent. Lacan clearly felt that the early Freud was not able to sustain an absolute distinction between the "two languages"; if they were really incommensurable, one language could not speak through the "other" and bring about analytic insight leading to a cure. The basis for this claim, however, extends beyond the clinic to what Lacan learned from Saussure, Levi-Strauss, and Jakobson about the ways that language in general functions. If all language did not work—fundamentally—in one way, namely through the difference between signifiers associated in chains, then there would be no possibility at all of attending to the discourse of the Other, of the unconscious subject. It is because Lacan has learned to think of all language as working in one way that he is able to challenge an absolute bifurcation between the language of conscious and unconscious thought. It is not a question, as in some forms of analysis, of replacing the language of the "blind id" with the language of the ego, aware of reality. It is rather a question of showing how, in analytical encounters, communication can occur between the two sides of the subject, the unconscious subject of desire and the conscious aspect of the ego, as well as between the two sides of the analyst's own subjectivity.

In the end, the difference between Lacan and Derrida reflects their different contexts—that of the clinic and that of philosophical reflection—and the different urgencies that position them. It is as important for Lacan to claim that all language works in a single more or less structuralist way in order to promote a cure as it is for Derrida to deny a unified theory of language in order to open up spacings—cuts, abysses, voids—between solidified and sedimented cultural and intellectual meanings.

Lacan, Religion and Psychology

Since the essays which follow are devoted, in varying ways, to an exploration of themes in religion, psychology, theology, and culture, it only remains, in conclusion, to suggest their importance for the dialogue between religion and psychology. In a broad sense, this dialogue begins in Western culture prior to the rise of psychology as an independent discipline. When Augustine, for example, at the origins of the Christian tradition, made discourse between God and *psyche* central to most of his texts, combining Neo-Platonic philosophical psychology with his pilgrim's understanding of faith seeking understanding, he made issues of mind—soul, psyche—in its relationship to God the substance of Western religious discourse. Aquinas's debate with the Latin Averroists on the agent intellect, and his argument for the independent act of existence of each soul, is another representative chapter in that extended discussion, as is Schleiermacher's debate with Hegel about the origin and structure of consciousness from the perspective of faith.

This broad context of the discussion between religion and psychology is at work in many of the texts in this volume. From the narrower perspective of contemporary students of psychology and religion, the dialogue takes on a more problematic character. Beginning with the "wars of science and religion" in the eighteenth century, a fundamental swerve or error took place. The model of dialogue was replaced among some leading thinkers on both sides with a confrontation between psychology, as a scientific discipline independent of philosophy, and religious faith as representative of traditional beliefs shrouded in mystification. From this perspective, psychology, which combines theological reflection and clinical experience, has been misperceived as a reductive science of the human subject threatening to displace religious belief. Much of the work of scholars who share the desire to overcome this misunderstanding is designed to show how different, complementary patterns of relationship between psychology and religion can strengthen, rather than undermine religion. In a recent address on this subject,[37] John McDargh, a representative of this perspective, summarizes some of the directions taken in the dialogue between religion and psychoanalytic psychology over the last seventy-five years. He provides a broad perspective on the major issues with his distinction between "Protestant" and "Catholic" models for the integration/confrontation between the two fields.

McDargh characterizes the "Catholic" response as concerned with the "diminishment of the human," based on its understanding of continuity between the human and divine order and its belief in a natural human capacity for the transcendent. In this tradition, an emphasis on human freedom or a natural capacity to respond to grace is central, and McDargh suggests ways in which the work of Catholic theologians Karl Rahner and Bernard Lonergan in theological anthropology can be construed as responses to the challenge presented by depth psychology. The "Protestant" emphasis, by contrast, has been more concerned about the diminishment of the divine than with the impoverishment of the human, and has tended "to employ psychological categories in such a way as to make clear the discontinuity between what is properly styled the human or psychological and what can only be accounted for by reference to that which exceeds us utterly, the reality of God."[38] McDargh argues that the future of either "Catholic" or "Protestant" theological uses of psychology will depend on whether theologians creatively respond to those developments within depth psychology that offer a way through the reductionism of an earlier psychological era. However, despite the title of the concluding section of his remarks, "Theology and Post-Modern Psychoanalysis: Prospects for a Partnership," McDargh's perspective remains essentially modern in its concern for the unity and coherence of the subject, as understood in the work of object-relations theorists and self-psychologists.

Here, one might suggest that the major impact of Lacan has thus far been limited primarily to those whose perspectives are influenced by theological/philosophical/literary critical considerations rather than clinical/cultural ones. This may be the result of the contrast between modernism and postmodernism, or between humanism and antihumanism. Modern perspectives originate in Descartes and Kant's "turn to the subject." They share a common humanistic concern to preserve the autonomy, integrity, and creativity of the subject—or of the mind, the psyche—against various forms of critical reductionism, whether critical-scientific (during the seventeenth and eighteenth centuries), or postcritical (during the nineteenth century). To the extent that liberal theology is based on Schleiermacher's displacement of the certainty of faith from an arena open to historical criticism into the interior of consciousness, the liberal theological tradition in both its Catholic and Protestant forms has a strong stake in this modern concern for modes of analysis that would preserve the integrity of consciousness. This tradition would also leave an opening within consciousness for the apprehension of the transcendent, of that which exceeds consciousness, however conceived. Kate Soper provides a useful definition of the distinction between the "humanism" of this modern, Anglo-American liberal perspective and the "antihumanism" which tends to be characteristic of those influenced by contemporary Continental thought:

> Humanism: appeals (positively) to the notion of a core humanity or common essential features in terms of which human beings can be defined and understood, thus (negatively) to concepts ('alienation', 'inauthenticity', 'reification', etc.) designating and intended to explain, the perversion or 'loss' of this common being. Humanism takes his-

tory to be a product of human thought and action, and thus claims that the categories of 'consciousness', 'agency', 'choice' 'responsibility', 'moral value', etc. are indispensable to its understanding.

Anti-humanism: claims that humanism as outlined above is pre-scientific 'philosophical anthropology'. All humanism is 'ideological'; the ideological status of humanism is to be explained in terms of the systems of thought or 'consciousness' produced in response to particular historical periods. Anthropology, if it is possible at all, is possible only on condition that it rejects the concept of the human subject'; 'men' do not make history, nor find their 'truth' or 'purpose' in it; history is a process without a subject.[39]

Those working within the conversation between religion and psychoanalytic theory who have a clinical orientation have tended to be shaped by this modern, humanistic, liberal theological tradition, and to gravitate towards those varieties of psychoanalytic theory that offer a means of restoring or repairing the self. The critical tools of psychoanalysis, in an analogue to classical theological/pastoral techniques of critical self-examination, are used to dissolve a false or partial self, with the ultimate aim of self-restoration. Hence one speaks of the discovery or recovery of an "archetypal Self" in Jungian and neo-Jungian psychology, or of the healing of the self in Kohut's self-psychology, in ways that link these healing processes with classical traditions' understandings of grace. If liberal theology has relocated the essence of religious belief within the psyche, modern approaches to religion and psychology can be construed as apologetic attempts to maintain the liberal humanistic legacy in the contemporary world. A return to the origins of faith is made possible through a return to the authentic origins of the self.

Those who have been influenced by Lacan, on the other hand, tend to adopt a postmodern perspective on the disappearance, dissolution, death, or dismemberment of the self, and to assume at least some validity in the antihumanist critique of humanism's mythologization and captivity to neopositivist ideologies. Such postmodern perspectives find their "origin" in the criticisms of the duplicity of consciousness launched by Nietzsche, Marx, and Freud, and the question is then how to understand those criticisms. Whereas Paul Ricoeur argues that "all three . . . far from being detractors of 'consciousness', aim at extending it,"[40] postmodern approaches to the subject insist on the critical aspects of the "hermeneutic of suspicion," that is, those that seem to dissolve or dismember the unity and coherence of the subject. The issues between these two perspectives on the subject are not confined to theory, nor, as Hal Foster shows, is it as simple as an argument between modernism and postmodernism: within the wide spectrum of discourses identified as "postmodern," there are at least two opposing strands or themes:

> In cultural politics today, a basic opposition exists between a postmodernism which seeks to deconstruct modernism and resist the status quo and a postmodernism which repudiates the former to celebrate the latter: a postmodernism of resistance and a postmodernism of reaction.[41]

Foster argues that while the postmodernism of reaction is in essence cosmetic, a mask for a return to the verities of tradition in art, family, or religion, a postmodernism of resistance is concerned for a critical deconstruction of tradition, a critique of origins, and "to explore rather than to conceal social and political affiliations [of various theoretical discourses]."[42] One of the major questions this volume opens up is whether essays such as those that follow can stimulate a conversation between the primarily liberal, humanistic, or modern theological-psychological approach of those with a theological/clinical orientation, and the radical, postmodern theological perspective of those whose attitudes have been shaped by philosophical, theological, and literary-critical concerns, and who seem committed to a postmodernism of resistance.

The postmodern emphasis on the dissolution of the self can—and sometimes does—claim a venerable religious heritage. One can cite the *anatta* doctrine of Theravada Buddhism, the assaults on self carried out in Zen Buddhism, or the tradition of the *via negativa* within the Christian tradition. But an important difference also needs to be noted. Classical, premodern critiques of the self are often meant to clear a space for a "higher" or "truer" self, as has been the case in Theravada Buddhism, and the same may be argued about the Western religious traditions, Protestant as well as Catholic. There is also, at least in Western if not in Eastern religion, the notion of God as a transcendent subject who supports and creates all other subjectivites. The critique of self-centeredness is intended to reveal the existential and ontological dependence of all created subjects upon God.

Clearly Lacan's work is critical of the ego as an alienating form of defense against desire. There is also in Lacan a notion of "another subject," the "subject of desire". The question here is whether in Lacan, as in some other forms of postmodern psychology, such as James Hillman's archetypal psychology,[43] the effect of critical questioning is to clear the way for a return to some form of *arche*, or origin. If so, the postmodern is a route through which to return to the (repressed?)

premodern — to what was before the Enlightenment and its critical legacy. But Lacan may also be seen as holding that Freud's legacy poses the inevitability and permanence of division within the self, which can neither be healed nor transformed: the origin is unavailable because it is before all possible language.

Is the space cleared by postmodernism one that allows for a return of grace — or is it a space in which, as the critics of postmodernism sometimes argue, nothing, no one, can live? This issue will not be resolved here. Not all of the authors agree about its importance — but this debate over whether the subject requires healing or dissolution is one place to begin the conversation.

On Writing About Writing About Lacan: A Conclusion

Readers who may wish to return to this introduction after a reading of the chapters that follow will note a major difference in style, about which a comment seems appropriate. In contrast to many of the essays, this introduction is deliberately nonplayful, and seeks to follow — more or less — the customary canons of exposition and ideals of clarity. Since much of what Lacan has to offer is presented in a style that is deliberately obfuscating, for reasons proposed earlier, this attempt at a lucid introduction or frame may seem a betrayal of his insight.

A similar dilemma is confronted by all would-be expositors of postmodern materials, whether in philosophy, literary criticism, or psychoanalytic theory and theology: whether the aim of reaching a wider audience justifies the risk of allowing that audience to think that it has captured what Lacan — or any other postmodern thinker — has to offer, after reading an organized, critical summary of that thinker's position. Enough has been indicated about the importance of the question of style in Lacan — in the Lacan-Derrida debate — to preclude such a possibility: one cannot "have" the text without the text!

One of the pervasive ironies of this volume is that just when the authors struggle most to return to what is mute, to what lies before the agency of letter, to desire or to the "active void" — in the spirit of Lacan's return to Freud and the "Freudian thing" — that they are the most "original", "creative," speaking the language of the Other but in their own, overdetermined voices. The attempt to create or, in some of the authors, to return through deconstruction toward a clearing in which that which is unspoken can be heard, may appear on first reading to have produced a thicket; but it is a clearing that is sought, nonetheless. Whether the clearing is full or empty, or, in the language of classical theology, gracious or demonic, is another question.

Notes

1. Joan Nordquist, comp., *Jacques Lacan: A Bibliography* (Santa Cruz: Reference and Research Services, 1987).

2. Juilet Flower MacCannell, *Figuring Lacan: Criticism and the Cultural Unconscious* (Lincoln: Nebraska University Press, 1986), 24.

3. Phillip Rieff, *The Triumph of the Therapeutic* (New York: Harper and Row, 1966).

4. Jules Henry, *Culture Against Man* (New York: Random House, 1963) and *Pathways to Madness* (New York: Random House, 1972).

5. Christopher Lasch, *The Culture of Narcissism: American Life in an Age of Diminishing Expectations* (New York: W.W. Norton, 1978). This book was ably criticized, among other places, in *Salmagundi*. See the essays by Michael Fisher, Larry D. Nachman, and Janice Doane and Devon Leigh Hodges, as well as Lasch's response, in Robert and Peggy Boyers, eds. *The Salmagundi Reader* (Bloomington: Indiana University Press, 1983), 152-88.

6. Richard Sennett, *The Fall of Public Man* (New York: Alfred A. Knopf, 1974).

7. Peter Homans, *Jung in Context: Modernity and the Making of a Psychology* (Chicago: University of Chicago Press, 1979). Don S. Browning discusses the American context of "psychology as culture" in his work on William James, *Pluralism and Personality* (Lewisburg, Pa.: Bucknell University Press, 1980), 20-42.

8. Homans, *Jung* 174-78; see also a major source cited by Homans on this topic, Salvador Giner, *Mass Society* (New York: Academic Press, 1976).

9. Robert N. Bellah, Richard Madsen, William M. Sullivan, Ann Swidler, and Steven M. Tipton, *Habits of the Heart* (New York: Harper and Row, 1985).

10. See, for example, Ernest Wallwork, "A Constructive Freudian Alternative to Psychotherapeutic Egoism," in *Soundings* 69, nos. 1-2 (Spring/Summer 1986): 145-64.

11. Guy M. Thompson, *The Death of Desire: A Study in Psychoanalysis* (New York: New York University Press, 1985), 60.

12. Holland first develops this notion in a volume edited by Ihab and Sally Hassan, *Innovation/Renovation: New Perspectives on the Humanities* (Madison: University of Wisconsin Press, 1983), 291-310. He has since expanded his discussion of postmodern psychoanalysis in *The I* (New Haven: Yale University Press, 1985).

13. This point has been clearly demonstrated in important essays by Edward Casey and J. Melvin Woody, and by Wilfried Ver Eeck, in Joseph H. Smith

and William Kerrigan, eds., *Interpreting Lacan* (New Haven: Yale University Press, 1983), 75-138. Lacan's debt to Hegel (and to Kojève's reading of Hegel) is also ably discussed by Anthony Wilden in his essay, "Lacan and the Discourse of the Other," in Jacques Lacan, *Speech and Language in Psychoanalysis* ed. Anthony Wilden (Baltimore: Johns Hopkins University Press, 1968), 192-96. Although not directed to Lacan's appropriation of Hegel, Rodolphe Gasche, *The Tain of the Mirror: Derrida and the Philosophy of Reflection* (Cambridge: Harvard University Press, 1986), provides a useful historical-conceptual introduction to a key Lacanian notion, reflexivity, in the first section of the book, "Toward the Limits of Reflection," 1-108.

14. Jacques Lacan, "The Unconscious: A Psychoanalytic Study," cited in Anika Lemaire, *Jacques Lacan* (London: Routledge and Kegan Paul, 1977), 167.

15. Jacques Lacan, *Ecrits*, cited in Lemaire, 168. For a further discussion of the importance of the "death drive," see "Why the Death Drive?" Chapter 6 of *Life and Death in Psychoanalysis*, by a leading Lacanian, Jean Laplanche (Baltimore: Johns Hopkins University Press, 1976).

16. See Victoria Hamilton, *Narcissus and Oedipus* (London: Routledge and Kegan Paul, 1982), 27-123. Hamilton makes no mention of Lacan in her typology. One can compare this curious neglect to Heinz Kohut's lack of reference to Lacan's "mirror stage" as a parallel to Kohut's important notion of mirroring internalization.

17. See Heinz Hartmann, *Ego Psychology and the Problem of Adaptation*, trans. David Rapaport. *Journal of the American Psychoanalytic Association*, Monograph No. 1. (New York: International Universities Press, 1958) for an introduction to those features of Hartmann's position to which Lacan objects.

18. "Narration in the Psychoanalytic Dialogue," in W.J.T. Mitchell, ed., *On Narrative* (Chicago: University of Chicago Press, 1981), 32, 48. See also Shafer's *A New Language for Psychoanalysis* (New Haven: Yale University Press, 1976).

19. Robert Con Davis, "Introduction: Lacan and Narration," in Robert Con Davis, ed., *Lacan and Narration: The Psychoanalytic Difference in Narrative Theory* (Baltimore: Johns Hopkins University Press, 1983), 853-54.

20. Heinz Kohut, *How Does Analysis Cure?* ed. Arnold Goldberg with the collaboration of Paul E. Stepansky (Chicago: University of Chicago Press, 1984), 96.

21. Ibid., 52.

22. Ibid., 103.

23. Thompson, *Death of Desire*, 12-13.

24. Ibid., 187.

25. Jeffrey Mehlman, "Trimethylamin: Notes on Freud's Specimen Dream," in Robert Young, ed., *Untying the Text: A Post-Structuralist Reader* (London: Routledge and Kegan Paul, 1981), 179.

26. Adolf Grunbaum, *The Foundations of Psychoanalysis: A Philosophical Critique* (Berkeley: University of California Press, 1984).

27. Ibid., 3, 6.

28. William Kerrigan, "Introduction," in J.H. Smith, and W. Kerrigan, *Interpreting Lacan*, 15. The relevant portion of Ricoeur's text notes that "for a philosophical critique [of Freud], the essential point concerns what I call the place of . . . energy discourse. Its place, it seems to me, lies at the intersection of desire and language; we will attempt to account for this place by an archeology of the subject." Paul Ricoeur, *Freud and Philosophy: An Essay on Interpretation* (New Haven: Yale University Press, 1970), 395. Ricoeur argues that Freud "focuses on a signifying power that is operative prior to language" (398) at a number of significant points in his work, and that while the Lacanian linguistic interpretation "has the merit of raising all phenomena of the primary process and of repression to the rank of language," the "distortion . . . which turns that other discourse into a quasi language is not itself achieved by language" (405).

29. John P. Muller and William J. Richardson, *Lacan and Language: A Reader's Guide to Ecrits* (New York: International Universities Press, 1982).

30. Ellie Ragland-Sullivan, *Jacques Lacan and the Philosophy of Psychoanalysis* (Urbana: University of Illinois Press, 1986), 211, 217, 221. The discussion of Lacan and language in Anika Lemaire's *Jacques Lacan*, by contrast, tends to place Lacan's work more closely within a structuralist context.

31. Derrida's concept of "writing before the letter" has been carefully examined in Gasché's, *The Tain of the Mirror*, cited above. Gasché proposes that "writing in Derrida's sense is not determined by what it is about, nor has it anything essentially in common with the signs present on the page, or with the (literary or philosophical) production of these signs. Neither is it the essence of the literal sign or of the act of its engendering. . . . It has no proper value of its own, positive or negative. Arche-writing is only, if one may say so, the quasitranscendental synthesis that accounts for the necessary corruption of idealities, or transcendentals of all sorts, by what they are defined against, and at the very moment of their constitution. . . . Rather than being the exterior double of speech, proto-writing is that synthetic structure of referral that accounts for the fact that in the play of differences between say, speech and writing, ideality and writing, meaning and writing . . . the pole allegedly present in and of itself, which allegedly refers to itself alone, must in fact constitute itself through the element it abases" (274-75). Robert Con Davis argues, *In Lacan and Narration*, that while "there is no knowable subject in Lacan's text or in Derrida's text (no Other of the Other) . . . the desire of the Other—[which is] not part of the

Derridean program — positions and limits the free play of signification through the continual resubjection of the signifier (the subject) to the Other's desire, through the continual 'passage into the semiotic triangle of Oedipus' " (855).

32. First published as Jacques Derrida, *Positions* (Les Editions de Minuit, 1972); English translation, under the same title,by Alan Bass (Chicago: University of Chicago Press, 1981).

33. First published in *Poetique* 21 in 1975, and subsequently republished as a chapter of *La Carte postale: De Socrate à Freud et au-delà* (Paris: Flammarion, 1980); English translation by Alan Bass, under the title, *The Post-Card* (Chicago: University of Chicago Press, 1987).

34. First published as *L'Oreille de l'autre*, ed. Claude Levesque and Christie V. McDonald, (V1b Editeur, Montreal, 1982). English translation *The Ear of the Other* by Peggy Kamuf (New York: Schocken Books, 1985).

35. *The Post Card*, 473-74.

36. *Positions*, 109-10.

37. John McDargh, "Theological Uses of Psychology: Retrospective and Prospective", unpublished MS delivered at The American Academy of Religion, 1986.

38. Ibid., 3.

39. Kate Soper, *Humanism and Anti-Humanism* (La Salle, IL.: Open Court, 1986), 11-12. See 120-30 for Soper's critical appraisal of Lacan based on her more general critique of "anti-humanism.".

40. In "Psychoanalysis and Contemporary Culture," in Paul Ricoeur, *The Conflict of Interpretations* (Evanston, Ill.: Northwestern University Press, 1974), 150.

41. Hal Foster, "Postmodernism: A Preface," in Hal Foster, ed., *The Anti-Aesthetic: Essays on Postmodern Culture* (Port Townsend, Wash.: Bay Press, 1983), xii.

42. Ibid.

43. James Hillman's archetypal psychology is a development within neo-Jungian rather than neo-Freudian thought that can provide a valuable benchmark for those interested in whether or to what extent Lacan is to be placed within the frame of postmodernism. As articulated in *The Myth of Analysis* (New York: Harper and Row, 1972); *Re-Visioning Psychology* (New York: Harper and Row, 1975); and *The Dream and the Underworld* (New York: Harper and Row, 1979), Hillman's position shows some similarities with Lacan's. Both are critical of the centrality of the ego in American psychoanalysis, and offer forms of therapy that seek to dissolve its illusions. Both are seen by representatives of Jungian and Freudian "orthodoxy" respec-

tively as radical and eccentric. This has led to Hillman's being identified by some with Lacan as "postmodern." A closer comparison shows the difference: Hillman draws extensively on premodern sources such as Gnosticism and Renaissance Neo-Platonism in his theory construction, and his emphasis on attending to the hermetic discourse of dreams—on "befriending dreams"—suggests an emphasis on the content of dream images that leads to forms of mystification and magic. Lacan, despite the oblique qualities of his style, is clearly engaged in a radical challenge to all forms of mysticism. Hillman's work is closer to a postmodernism of reaction than of resistance, which illustrates the importance of the precise use of labels in discussing "postmodern" forms of psychoanalytic theory.

1.

Lacan and Theological Discourse

Charles E. Winquist

In "Deconstructing Theology," part one of Mark Taylor's book *Erring*, he examines four losses for postmodern theological thinking: (1) the death of God, (2) the disappearance of the self, (3) the end of history, and (4) the closure of the book. The interdependence of the concepts of God, self, history, and book means that the death, disappearance, end, or closure of any of these concepts would have implications that can be traced throughout the dissemination of the others. It was the proclamation of the death of God by Nietzsche's madman, sustained throughout the vagaries of twentieth century American theology, that has received the most immediate attention in theological discourse. Through a variety of hermeneutical strategies, the God of faith seems to have survived the radical theologies of the sixties, but I would like to suggest that these strategies have a confidence in the integrity of self-understanding, hope in historical processes, or belief in a holism or sometimes even totalization of thinking. It is precisely this confidence, hope, or belief that is insidiously undermined in the implicate disorder brought by radical theological thinking.

As Ricoeur and others have noted, it is not just Nietzsche who is a discordant voice of suspicion from the nineteenth century, forcing a rethinking of thinking in the twentieth century; we must also attend to Freud and Marx. I would like to suggest that the relevance of a turn to Jacques Lacan and theological discourse is a return to Freud and, most importantly, a return to what is unassimilable in Freud. It is Lacan's understanding of the subversion of the subject in Freud (what Taylor calls the disappearance of the self) that has severe implications for any theory of theological discourse. It is a move behind the adaptive strategies of Americanized ego-psychologies to originary wounds where the "it" of the unconscious is marked.

What we first notice when we turn to Lacan and the secondary literature about the work and life of Lacan is that everyone has trouble reading Lacan. Muller and Richardson "call Lacan's writings a rebus.

26

... Lacan not only explicates the unconscious but strives to imitate it.[1] We have no simple understanding of "Who is speaking?" when we read Lacan. We do not simply interrogate the text but we are interrogated by the text. This belongs to style. Lacan is teaching style. Jane Gallop suggests that Lacan's *Ecrits* are writerly texts—"written not to be read."[2] The reader is implicated in a perpetual struggle of production. It is not a benign *agon*. The rebus is not a parlor-game puzzle that is to be undone or put together. In reading Lacan we assume our inevitable castration in language.[3] Lacan's style is "the man to whom one addresses oneself" and as Gallop suggests, "the violence of Lacan's style is its capacity to make the reader feel nonidentical with herself as reader ... to make the reader feel inadequate to her role as 'the man to whom Lacan addresses himself,' that is, inadequate to Lacan's style."[4]

Lacan develops a style of analytical discourse that fixates a concept of the subversion of the subject that is at the same time an oxymoronic requirement for slippage in speech and writing, leaving cuts, gaps, and spaces on the recording surface of experience. Reading Lacan is a lesson in Lacanian reading. A Lacanian reading is not a search for hidden significations but is an insistence on the letter of the text in the specific dialectic of text production. It would be a shallow misreading of Lacan to begin to search for specific Lacanian concepts in a theological text. The real loss in a theological assimilation of Lacanian concepts would be the loss of the loss we experience in Lacanian discourse. When theological concepts are used to mirror rather than interrogate reality, the unrestricted scope of these concepts can transumptively relocate figurations of lack on a surface that seems to fill in the lack. For example, Lacan's formula for atheism, "God is unconscious," can be psychologically tamed if it is relocated from the Freudian unassimilable "it" into a confident discourse of theological consciousness-raising. Here, there would be a falling back on a specular figure of wholeness so that when the "it" of the unconscious God is remarked in symbolic discourse, it has been or could have been transposed into a different discursive situation that is not Lacanian. This possible scenario is better understood by examining Lacan's notions of orders of the imaginary, symbolic, and real and their relationships to the mirror stage.

Sometime in that interval of infancy between six and eighteen months, the child is able to recognize its own image in a mirror. The mirror stage is an identification and marks a transformation of the subject when the subject assumes an image. As Lacan says, "the *I* is precipitated in a primordial form."[5] A substitution occurs. The love of the image of the whole body is substituted for the autoerotic relationship to the partial objects of the fragmented body. The subject is separated from the primacy of perception of the fragmented body in the reflection of the primordial image of a whole body. The mirror image can be thought of as a referential fantasy or imago for a transcendental unity of apperception that is outside of the subject. This unification and totalization of form is virtual and alienated. The mirror image cannot be touched. Only the mirror can be touched. The image can be indexed only on an imaginary register. The mirror image is the reflection of a projection and, as such, is the privileged experience of structuring projections. The subject transcends and loses the molecular multiplicity of the subject. There is an imaginary mastery in the naming and idealistic unification of the image. The mirror is a surface and the image can be unified and total and have no depth. The surface of the mirror is a recording surface that lacks depth, lacks organs, lacks being.

It is in the mirror stage that the subject is reified as an image outside of intersubjective structures that are themselves a play of differences. The order of the imaginary becomes a realm where the play of differences is covered over by mirroring.[6] This appears to be a heuristic qualification to help explain how a tendency toward idealization can have empirical credibility. As Gallop says, "Lacan's writings contain an implicit ethical imperative to break the mirror, an imperative to disrupt the imaginary in order to reach the symbolic."[7] She goes on to suggest that the symbolic can only be reached as a tear in the fabric of the imaginary.[8] The move to the symbolic register is through the imaginary. When the imaginary is understood to be imaginary and not an empirical refuge, it is then located in a discursive situation that is intersubjective and differential. The imaginary experience is linked to the symbolic order as soon as it is given over to discourse. What is imaginary has voice in the symbolic order if it is to be anything other than a mute repetition of its scene of origination. The identification of the imaginary order with the mirror stage and the accession to the symbolic can be understood as a strategy for differentiating language and symbolic discourse from a mimetic function. The goal of thinking is not an adaptation to the order of the real, because the domain of the real is outside of the representation of the subject, be it through the imaginary ego or through the representational play of the symbolic. The truth of the subject is found in the locus of the Other.

This claim makes sense only if we see how Lacan understands a differential play in the symbolic order. It is here that we also see the originality of Lacan's use of linguistics to articulate his return to what is unassimilable in Freud. Lacan accepts the Saussurian distinction between the signifier and the signified. Meaning is made determinate in the interrelationship and play of differences between signifiers. The signified is itself in a web of signification which is always a play of signifiers. Unlike Saussure, Lacan emphasizes the bar separating the signifiers from the signified. The circle or ellipse that embraces and unifies the Saussurrian algorithmic expression of the barred relationship between signifier and signified is erased. The signified is absent in the present play of signifiers. There is no mimetic reference to the real. The bar is an aporia. Identity is in difference. The symbolic order is the possibility for deferral and difference. This is what it means to represent an identity.

The Lacanian algorithm is a formula of separateness that does not admit of a reciprocity between the signifiers and the signified. This has a remarkable implication for the representation of the Freudian unconscious. "The unconscious is structured like a language."[9] We are never conscious of the unconscious as unconscious. It can only be known in an overdeterminate structure of language manifested symptomatically. The unconscious must be structured like a language, a play of signifiers, to have the referential motility that characterizes its formations. This is a consideration of representability. Lacan says that the linguistic structure "assures us that there is, beneath the term unconscious, something definable, accessible and objectifiable."[10] This is not the Freudian unconsciousness but it does designate that it is in the symbolic order that we will encounter the unconscious. It will be in the symbolic order that the written or spoken sentence will stumble. There will be gaps and as Lacan understands Freud, "the discovery is in these gaps.[11]

What is discovered is not what is present. What is discovered is an absence. Quoting from Lacan, "the reality of the unconscious . . . is not an ambiguity of acts, future knowledge that is already known not to be known, but lacuna, cut, rupture inscribed in a certain lack."[12] The unconscious is what is unthought in thinking. It is where the fabric of the text gapes. It is in the sensuality of the trace . . . in what appears through what disappears. We might say that Lacan's return to Freud is a return of the repressed. We are back to the it of the unconscious, and it is anticonceptual and thus unassimilable. It resides in a domain that is always other. Repression delineates a domain of otherness.

There is a possible trap in this language that could lead to a theological misreading of Lacan. When Lacan talks about the grand Other, there is a temptation to objectify the other and name it God. It is then too easy to fill in the gap that is the importance of otherness. Lacan is concerned about the subject. The other is an object of the interrogation of the subject — "Who is speaking?" The interrogation of the Other reveals a lack. The Other is barred as the subject is barred. There is an otherness that represents what the grand Other lacks. In the phenome-

nality of the representation of desire the lack is the petite other of
partial objects—an anus, a nipple, feces, the gaze, the phoneme, the
nothing.[13] These petite objects do not represent a whole; they are
what escapes the subject. They are the lack in the grand Other. They
are the lack in the Other that constitutes the subject as subject. The
limit of the unconscious is the concept of lack.[14] One cannot build a
positive science of theology on this notion of the Other—on this notion
of the unconscious.

Theology will not be a phenomenology describing otherness. That
would be a catalogue of partial objects marking a lack, a loss, and
constituting a desire. A theology responsive to Lacan will be a theology of desire unless it delimits its own interrogative structure. That is,
what we encounter in Lacan that is immediately relevant for any theory of theological discourse is that its speech will always speak a lack
and that the domain of its discourse is barred so that the otherness of
reality does not belong to description but to desire. Theology must
develop strategies of desire in language. We have returned to the question of style, which is where we began, because to think Lacan is to
think style.

What we need is an articulation of textual strategies that accept
responsibility in their own reflexivity for the repression of otherness.
These are textual strategies that do not compensate for loss by a fascination with exotica but work through themselves toward the significance of otherness. Desire references what discourse is not but it is
only known discursively. The problematic of desire in language is to
acknowledge extralinguistic reference and yet stay within an internal
play of linguistic signification.

It is here that we can discern a new warrant for theological thinking and place its importance within the study of religion. Theological
thinking is relevant because it is other than ordinary discourse and is
itself a discourse that can display the otherness of its semantic achievement. This is already part of the achievement of the theological tradition.
Historically the fundament in theology has been unrestricted—God,
ultimate reality, Brahman, and other unrestricted formulations—and
even though an objective and descriptive literalism is no longer credible, the definition of theology as a discursive discipline includes responsibility for unrestricted inquiry. Notions of "that than which nothing
greater can be conceived" violate intelligible closure to achievements
of understanding within the symbolic order. We could characterize theology as a deconstructive agent and theological thinking as a deconstructive act within the symbolic order.

A post-Lacanian theology would not be defined by the object of
its inquiry. What was in the center of theological thinking and why

theology was itself in the center of intellectual inquiry is now marked by a lack and a loss. Theology harbors no secret knowledge and has no access to a hidden order of things. It must be like a nomad wandering over the surface of the symbolic and imaginary orders. However, what it does not surrender in its diverse losses is its unrestricted interrogative form. Its conceptual formulations instantiate a radical negativity simply by being thought. Questions about what we take seriously without any reservation may not have answers but they transgress the boundaries of semiotic captivity.

This means that theology is textual production in which the author is written into the work as a theologian by implicating the text in the exigencies of the unrestricted scope of theological inquiry. We still will be reading a text, but the text will be marked and sometimes re-marked by fissures wrought by limiting questions, poetic indirections, and figures of brokenness. From its marginal position theological inverbalization and inscription will be a supplement to ordinary thinking. We might even think of theology as a supplementary valuation of the otherness that is present only by its absence in the textual articulation of experience. It is, in its postmodern articulation, a method of hesitation on the surface, the fold, the skin, and the appearance of reality, so that there can be an acute recognition of our being there in the world. There is in this recognition a consent to an otherness of reality—a primal sense of nature—that is always in danger of being repressed and exploited by systems of thinking.

Theological defamiliarization can be understood as an ethical experiment in letting things be in their otherness. It works against the conformation of the natural to the idealization of intellectual systems. It is in particular a lever of intervention from within language that prevents symbol systems from pretending closure. This is important because language can cover up its forgetfulness unless there is a commitment to subvert the closure of language from within language. The trajectory of the theological use of language is not the representation of God. It is, instead, as Scharlemann has suggested in "The Being of God When God Is Not Being God," the instantiation of a radical negativity that marks the otherness of the subject or object of discourse. When the word God is allowed to function in a radical defamiliarization of the subject and object of discourse, the strategy of theological thinking is reflexive. Language subverts itself in this dialectical release of language to its otherness. Theology is then both in and out of language, even though "the referent of theological meaning is given in and as language."

In this revision of the theological task, systematic theology can never come to completion and foundational theology is not a meta-analysis.

Theology cannot stand outside of itself to envision its radical possibilities. One of the implications for situating foundational theology in relation to a Lacanian theory of discourse is that theology is necessarily radical. That is, it is reflexive. It turns on itself toward its own roots. Its radical possibilities are an achievement of its internal subversion. It cannot become a system because it works against the completeness of a system.

Theological thinking is an ongoing experiment. It may be an experiment with the truth, but it is more importantly an experiment of desire. Theology, with its radical conceptuality, implicates desire in the full range of textual achievements. If we return to those characteristics of a postmodern theology defined by Mark Taylor—the death of God, the disappearance of the self, the end of history, and the closure of the book—we see that even if we look hard at any one of these losses, theology still has a task. The theological exigency in thinking has not been lost. Instead it has a special role in its capacity to transgress any closure of the symbolic order. It is its complexification of the symbolic order and its transgression that references the depth of experience as desire.

Lacan is an ally of theology because he forces theology to seriously assess the problematic of its own textuality. Reading Lacan helps us understand theology as a formal radicalization of reading. Theology becomes a reflexive rather than reflective engagement with reality.

Notes

1. John P. Muller and William J. Richardson, *Lacan and Language: A Reader's Guide to Ecrits* (New York: International Universities Press, 1982), 3.

2. Jane Gallop, *Reading Lacan* (Ithaca, N.Y.: Cornell University Press, 1985), 46.

3. Ibid., 20.

4. Ibid., 117.

5. Jacques Lacan, *Ecrits: A Selection*, trans. Alan Sheridan (New York: W.W. Norton, 1977), 2.

6. Gallop, *Reading Lacan*, 59.

7. Ibid.

8. Ibid., 60.

9. Jacques Lacan, *The Four Fundamental Concepts of Psychoanalysis*, trans. Alan Sheridan (New York: W.W. Norton, 1978), 20.

10. Ibid., 21.

11. Ibid., 25.

12. Ibid., 153.

13. Lacan, *Ecrits*, 315.

14. Lacan, *Four Fundamental Concepts*, 26.

Works Cited

Gallop, Jane. *Reading Lacan*. Ithaca: Cornell University Press, 1985.

Lacan, Jacques. *Ecrits: A Selection*. Trans. Alan Sheridan. New York: W.W. Norton, 1977.

_____. *The Four Fundamental Concepts of Psychoanalysis*. Trans. Alan Sheridan. New York: W.W. Norton, 1978.

Muller, John P. and William J. Richardson. *Lacan and Language: A Reader's Guide to Ecrits*. New York: International Universities Press, 1982.

Summary

David Crownfield

Charles Winquist begins by situating his discussion in the context of Mark Taylor's deconstructive a/theology, and its focal attention to the death of God, the disappearance of the self, the end of history, and the closure of the book. It is primarily the role of Lacan in the disappearance of the self and the consequent reformulation of the nature of theological discourse that focuses this essay.

This self, already subverted in Marx, Nietsche, and Freud, is seen especially in Lacan to be nonidentical with itself. Both the author and the reader of Lacanian text are subverted, nonidentical, as an effect of a style nearly as enigmatic as we are ourselves. In our emergence from infancy, the fragmentation of the perceptual body is displaced by the "referential fantasy" of the mirror image of ourselves (not always literally a mirror; often Mother's regard). This reified, imaginary self that we can never touch, never possess, purports to unify — but inaccessibly — the intersubjective play of differences in symbolic (interpersonally signifying) language.

In Lacan, as in Saussure, meaning is determined in that play of differences between signifiers, a web to catch the signified. But the bar that in Saussure's notation unites the two sides of a unitary signification becomes for Lacan the marker of the ever-elusive passage from signifier to world, infinitely deferred into one more difference between signifiers. (Winquist's reading of Lacan here is obviously aided by Derrida, but in a way that serves him well to get at what Lacan's play with the bar seems to be up to.)

It is within the symbolic order, in the deformation, stumbling, gaps, absences in the web of signifiers, that the unconscious is manifested. (In a sense, the unconscious resides in the symbolic, in the discourse of the individual, as this lack and deformation itself: it is that part of the language that signifies by its marked absence.) It is the unthought, as the unsaid or missaid. As such it is a domain of otherness.

Desire is the aim toward that other, that lack, the other side of the bar: "Desire references what discourse is not but it is only known discursively. The problematic of desire is to acknowledge extralinguistic reference and yet stay within an internal play of linguistic significa- tion." It is in complexification and transgression of the symbolic order that (theological) discourse references the depth of experience as desire. (There is a problem here that Winquist has not addressed. As the aim toward the lack in discourse, desire is inherently unfulfillable for Lacan, is fundamentally illusory: its primordial intentionality is to the mirror self, to the phallus, to Mother: the unattainable. Winquist's characteri- zation of desire, as a depth of experience referenced by theological discourse, would appear to be at odds with Lacan's emphasis on its illusory essence.

Neither in the imaginary domain of the mirror-self nor in the inter- subjective and differential play of the symbolic do we find the truth of the subject, but in the locus of the Other—precisely as Other, as unattainable. But this Other is not to be objectified as God. Who is this Other? Not the objectified, which is signified only in order to be itself a signifier of the Other. The question points to a lack, marked or signified by partial objects (*objet petit a*). This lack is imagined as a lack in the Other, a desire of the Other, around which the subject seeks to constitute itself as subject. It is necessary to be careful here: on Lacanian ground nothing really does or can constitute the subject as subject. The lack in the Other is the fantasy lack that constitutes the Other's desire, on the basis of which I imagine myself as the object of that desire. In that sense it constitutes the subject, but once again as illusion: my desire, which is illusory, is a desire to be the object of the Other's desire, which is illusory, and creates an imaginary self as mirrored in that imagined desire. Winquist is, of course, quite right that this does not authorize an equation of Other with God, or a theological dis- course that would representationally signify an Other who can satisfy my desire.

In this perspective (and this is the heart of Winquist's proposal), theological discourse can only speak a lack, a barred domain. The oth- erness of reality figures in it as object not of description but of desire; theology must develop strategies of desire in language. Such a dis- course will reflexively accept responsibility for the repression of other- ness, devise textual strategies that mark (without possessing) the significance of otherness, acknowledge reference while remaining in the play of signification. It is the nonordinary otherness of theological discourse that is its warrant and indeed its definition: its relevance is in its display of the otherness of its own semantic achievement. (Thus, for example, Winquist reads Anselm's Ontological Argument as iconoclastic.) While there is no unrestricted object for theological discourse, it exists as a responsibility for unrestricted inquiry, deconstructive, erring, transgressing freely the symbolic/imaginary difference, writing the author into the work, self-marginalizing, a supplement, a hesitation, fold, skin, fissuring the text with limiting questions, indirections, figures of brokenness.

This unlimited discourse marks in its inability to articulate the otherness of reality the trace of that otherness itself, accomplishing this by these fissures, subversions of the closure of language, tactics of defamiliarization. It is the instantiation of a radical negativity: in this role the word *God* can function reflexively and subversively. Theological discourse thus is an experiment of desire, a radicalization of reading, a reflexive engagement with reality.

The provocations and suggestions in this argument are fruitful and revelatory. Yet there are questions that I think need a careful look further, that would call perhaps for a different treatment. Two critical questions are the matter of desire as illusory, which I have mentioned above, and the problem of the *theological* character of this open, interrogative, deconstructive discourse. Clearly it is intended to be, in Taylor's sense, a/theological; equally clearly, it cannot in this context be required to justify itself by reinstating some referential theism. But is there not a connection, besides the boundless negativity of iconoclasm, between the already extant practices and texts of theological discourse and the decision to call this unlimited discourse theological? If so, why is that connection silent in Winquist's discussions? Is this a signifying silence, a mark of the unsaid and unthought, of the repressed? If so, how can we bring it to thought, to speech? (Lacan said that the function of psychoanalysis is to teach the analysand the language of her/his desire. Can we find a language of desire for this lack?)

This, I think, is closely related to the problem of Winquist's treatment of desire in Lacan and in theology. If desire is empty, essentially impossible of fulfillment, deforming discourse in pursuit of that which is unattainable not only because it is outside speech but because it is unreal, an artifact of self-formation and signification—then to find theology its warrant as an experiment of desire, a development of strategies of desire in language, thus "referencing by transgression the depth of experience as desire," is to locate theological discourse precisely and squarely in the pathology of the symbolic, in regression to the imaginary.

Why does theological discourse, which already occurs, require a warrant at all? Why does its warrant make it over into something not visibly much like its actual and ordinary occurences? Who does Winquist desire to do theology, to do it differently, and to warrant it (even in a deconstructive mode)? Is this "warrant" a sort of phallus that will complete the body of the theologian, legitimate a mirror-subject as object of the other's desire, secure the connection of signification to the real, or what?

One aspect of Lacan's work that is missing here is the idea of the Law of the Father, or name (*nom   non*) of the father. Access to the symbolic order is based on the fact that the place of the father (not the person or the behavior of the father) marks the impossibility of union with mother or with the mirror-self. The phallus is the original signifier of this impossibility, and is thus the foundation of the whole scene of metonymic displacement and metaphoric substitution (corresponding to the displacements and condensations of Freudian primary process) that constitutes language itself. The decisive passage to post-infant existence is the submission to the law of substitution and displacement, to the unattainability of primary desire.

I find Winquist's image of theology as a strategy of desire consistent with his characterization of it as unconstrained interrogation: both formulations locate theological discourse in the refusal of the Law of the Father, in the imaginary, in the isolation of a solitary and marginal wanderer without context or community. But it is not in unconstrained difference but in the law of specific and shared contrasts that discourse achieves meaning; it is not in the ruptures that reference the inescapable persistence of the impossible dream of desire, but in the accepted and shared substitutes for desire that language does what it does.

Even read deconstructively and psychoanalytically, I want to maintain, there is no thinking or writing outside of tradition and community. Specifically not for theology.

2.

Refusal of the Bar

Mark C. Taylor

I begin with questions: What is an open bar? What would happen if the bar were open or opened? What is a closed bar? What happens when the bar is closed? What is the refusal of a closed bar? What is the refuse of a closed bar? What would it mean to re-fuse an open bar? What would it mean to refuse the closure of the bar?

These are not easy questions. The terms themselves are slippery: bar, barring, barred; refuse, refuse, re-fuse, of, of. As the meanings of these words unfold, the questions implied in the "Refusal of the Bar" proliferate. In what follows, I would like to consider briefly a question that often is barred: the question of the subject. The subject of my question is, then, the question of the subject. More precisely, my question concerns the implications of the barring of the subject or of the barred subject for thinking about *the law*.

It is impossible to consider the notion of the law apart from the matrix of concepts within which it assumes determinate form. That matrix is, at least in part, theological. Within the Western ontotheological tradition, the law is inseparably bound up with its "author" – God. If, as Nietzsche insists, God is dead, perhaps *the* law has reached a certain closure. The transition from God to law, or from the death of God to the end of *the* law is not direct but passes through the subject. The human subject is, in Michel Foucault's terms, "a theological conception." God and self are two sides of the same coin; each mirrors and is mirrored by the other. The leading death-of-God theologian, Thomas J.J. Altizer underscores the importance of Foucault's insight when he argues that "it was not until that period in Western history when God was fully manifest as being wholly isolated and apart that man discovered himself as an absolutely unique and autonomous being. . . . Only here and nowhere else in history do we find the conjunction of God appearing to consciousness as apart and beyond, and self-consciousness appearing to itself as its own individual and unique creator."[1]

The theology of the subject comes to fullest expression in modern philosophy, which "begins" with Descartes's inward turn and "ends" with Hegel's systematic exposition of the "absolute subject." Contrary to expectation, Hegel's philosophy of the subject harbors the seeds of its own dissolution. In the work of leading postmodern artists, writers, and theorists, the impossibility of Hegel's project becomes apparent. The significance of the critique of Hegel's system far surpasses the overthrow of yet another philosophical vision. In many ways, Hegelian philosophy represents the most complete articulation of dreams and aspirations that have always guided Western philosophers. Furthermore, it has become increasingly evident that philosophy is not an isolated discipline but stands in a thoroughly symbiotic relation to the society and culture within which it takes form. If, as Heidegger contends, Hegel's system constitutes "the end of philosophy" or is, as Derrida maintains, "the closure of metaphysics," then it might be necessary to reexamine the institutions that both shaped and have been shaped by the founding assumptions of western philosophy and metaphysics. Surely one of the most important and complex of these institutions is the law. In order to suggest *one* way in which such a reconsideration might begin, I would like to explore certain aspects of Lacan's subversive rereading of Hegel. In the barred subject of Lacanian analysis, questions that bear on the "refusal of the bar" become unavoidable.

In an effort to reconcile the opposites rending nature and history, Hegel argues that absolute spirit develops historically in what Milan Kundera derisively labels "The Grand March." This Grand March, which is supposed to lead to the fulfillment or satisfaction of human and divine spirit, falls into four major stages that Hegel describes, alternatively, in geographical language and in terms of the unfolding of the human life cycle. As spirit moves from the East, through Greece and Rome, to Germany, it progresses from infancy, through adolescence and manhood, to the maturity of old age. In *The Philosophy of History*, Hegel uses richly metaphorical terms to describe this movement:

> The *Sun* — the Light — rises in the East. . . . Imagination has often pictured to itself the emotions of a blind man suddenly becoming possessed of sight, beholding the bright glimmering of the dawn, the growing light, and the flaming glory of the ascending sun. The boundless forgetfulness of his individuality in this pure splendor is his first feeling — utter astonishment. But when the sun is risen, this astonishment is diminished; objects around are perceived, and from them the individual proceeds to the comprehension of his own inner being, and thereby the advance is made to the perception of the relation

between the two. Then inactive contemplation is left for activity; by the close of the day man has erected a building constructed from his own inner sun; and when in the evening he contemplates this, he esteems it more highly than the original external sun. For now he stands in a *conscious relation* to his spirit, and therefore a *free* relation. If we hold this image in mind, we shall find it symbolizing the course of history, the great day's work of spirit. The history of the world travels from East to West, for Europe is absolutely the end of history.[2]

In this westward movement, spirit progresses from an undifferentiated identity in which differences are not articulated, through the emergence of individuality and opposition among individuals, to a reintegration of particularity and difference within an all-encompassing organic totality. Two stages in this process are of special interest in this context: manhood (the Roman world) and maturity (the German world).

What constitutes "manhood (*Mannesalter*)" in The Grand March of history? The Roman world, according to Hegel, is guided by "the principle of abstract subjectivity," which presides over the cultivation of individual personality. With the breakdown of the primal harmony that Hegel, along with other Romantics, projects back into the Greek polis, individual subjects emerge in conflict with each other and over against both the divine personality and the transcendent deity's earthly representative, the emperor. The twin pillars that ground the individuality of the subject are private right and property. When fully developed, however, private right and property reverse the principle of "abstract subjectivity".

> We observed the Romans proceeding from the principle of abstract subjectivity, which now realizes itself in the recognition of private right. Private right, is this, viz., that the social unity as such enjoys consideration in the state, in the reality which he gives to himself— viz., in property. The living political body—that Roman feeling which animated it as its soul—is now brought back to the isolation of a lifeless private right. As, when the physical body suffers dissolution and each point gains a life of its own—a life that is only the miserable life of worms, so the political organism is here dissolved into atoms— viz., private persons. Such a condition is Roman life in this epoch: on the one side, fate and the abstract universality of sovereignty; on the other, the *individual* abstraction, 'Person', which involves the recognition of the independent dignity of the social unit—not on the ground of the display of the life which he possesses—in his complete individuality—but as the abstract *individuum*.[3]

Through a dialectical reversal, the decay of the social body in the conflict of atomistic individuals creates the possibility for spirit to come to maturity in the German world.

In contrast to nature, where "old age" is weakness, spiritual maturity is marked by "*strength*" in which destructive conflict finally is overcome. "Spirit," Hegel explains, "is the one, totally self-equal infinite, the pure identity [*die reine Identität*], which secondly separates itself from itself, as the other of its own self, as being for-itself and in-itself over against the universal. But this separation is sublated by the fact that atomistic subjectivity [*die atomistische Subjectivität*], as the simple relation to itself, is itself the universal, the identical with itself . . . For spirit posits itself as its other [*als sein Anderes*] and is the return to itself from this difference."[4] Spirit struggles to overcome all opposition by transforming every shape of otherness into "its own" or into "its own other." In terms of the *Phenomenology of Spirit*, spirit is "*other-being* and *being-for-self*, and in this determinateness, or in its self-externality, abides within itself; in other words, it is *in and for itself*."[5] The sublation of otherness, be that other religious, psychological, or sociopolitical, is the consistent aim of the modern philosophy of the subject. This philosophy of subjectivity is a philosophy of self-consciousness. Hegel's absolute knowledge is total self-consciousness, which he describes as "*Pure* self-recognition in absolute otherness."[6] When other mirrors self, difference is mastered and the subject appears to come into full possession of its proper identity. Such masterful self-possession marks the end, that is, the *telos* as well as the conclusion, of western philosophy and history.

Or so it seems. Thinkers from Kierkegaard and Marx to Deleuze and Derrida question the closure of Hegel's system. In an interview conducted in 1971, Derrida comments:

> In effect I believe that the Hegelian text is necessarily fissured; that it is something more and other than the circular closure of its representation. It is not reduced to a content of philosophemes, it also necessarily produces a powerful writing operation, a remainder of writing, whose strange relationship to the philosophical content of the Hegelian text must be reexamined, that is, the movement by means of which his text exceeds its meaning, permits itself to be turned away from, to return to, and to repeat itself outside its self-identity.[7]

The "something more and other" to which Derrida points entails precisely the otherness that Hegel's entire philosophy is constructed to dominate, master, and repress. If the Hegelian text is actually faulted, it is necessary to reexamine the modern philosophy of the subject.

One of the richest interrogations of the totalizing implications of Hegelian dialectics is developed in Lacan's rereading of Freud. Rather than attacking Hegel from without, Lacan approaches the System as if from within in order to expose the scene of the Other that forever haunts the Hegelian edifice. Like so many of his generation, Lacan was deeply influenced by Kojève's lectures on Hegel.[8] In contrast to someone like Merleau-Ponty, for whom Kojève's idiosyncratic reading of Hegel creates the possibility of "explor[ing] the irrational and integrat-[ing] it into an expanded reason,"[9] Lacan is persuaded that the Hegelian project is *impossible*. Reason can never be expanded sufficiently to integrate the irrational without remainder. The modern philosophy of subjectivity, which culminates in Hegel's analysis of absolute self-consciousness, founders on the *irreducible* unconscious discovered by Freud. In a deliberate effort to subvert the modern interpretation of the subject, Lacan formulates what might be understood as something like an anti-Cartesian, and by extension, anti-Hegelian motto for his undertaking: "I think where I am not, therefore I am where I do not think."[10] If "I am where I do not think," total self-consciousness is impossible. To begin to see why Lacan insists on the impossibility of transparent self-consciousness, it is necessary to examine the first part of his motto.

Before assaying an explanation of what Lacan means when he asserts, "I think where I am not", it is necessary to ask what he means by "I." What exactly is this "I" that is not? I have stressed that for Hegel, subjectivity comes to full realization in absolute knowledge. "This knowing," he explains, "is a pure *being-for-self* of self-consciousness; it is 'I', that is, *this* and no other 'I', and that is no less immediately a *mediated* or sublated *universal* 'I'. It has a *content* that it *differentiates* from itself; for it is pure negativity or the bifurcation of itself, it is *consciousness*. In its difference, this content is itself the "I', for it is the movement of sublating itself, or the same pure negativity that the 'I' is. In it, as differentiated, the 'I' is reflected into itself; the content is *comprehended* only when the 'I' is at home with itself in its being other."[11] Since the subject becomes itself *only* in and through the relationship to "its own other," the I is thoroughly social. In Hegel's phenomenology of spirit, the I first emerges when the desiring subject seeks satisfaction by engaging in a struggle for recognition. The desire that initiates and sustains the development of the subject is not satisfied until the I "is at home with itself in its being other."

Lacan attempts to demonstrate the impossibility of transparent self-consciousness by turning Hegel's argument against itself. In his well-known essay, "The Mirror Stage as Formative of the Function of the I as Revealed in Psychoanalytic Experience," Lacan uses Hegel's analysis of the reflective/reflexive relation of self and other in the struggle for

recognition to demonstrate that the I, understood as a perduring integrated ego, is a "specular image" that the infant first encounters in the
gaze of other subjects. The imaginary character of the I "situates the
agency of the ego . . . in a fictional direction, which will always remain
irreducible for the individual alone, or rather, which will only rejoin
the coming-into-being [le devenir] of the subject asymptotically, whatever the success of the dialectical syntheses by which he must resolve
as I his discordance with his own reality."[12] Contrary to Hegel's claim
that the I is fully realized (and thus desire satisfied) in complete self-
consciousness, Lacan contends that the subject is *always* incomplete
and desire *never* satisfied. The impossibility of complete self-consciousness implies that "I think where I am not" or, conversely, that I am not
where I think. "The formation of the I as we experience it in psychoanalysis," Lacan argues, "is an experience that leads us to oppose any
philosophy directly issuing from the *Cogito*."[13]

Since desire cannot be totally satisfied, the wound that Hegel tries
to heal remains open. The subject, in other words, is inevitably "split."
This fissure is not secondary or consequent to a more primary or original unity and integrity. To the contrary, the subject is always already
split. This split opens the "empty" space and "vacant" time of desire.
As a follower of Freud, Lacan is convinced that desire can be neither
truly known nor directly expressed. Always subject to detours and
delays, desire is forever barred. This barring is, in effect, a refusal of
refuse that can never be re-fused. The barring of desire results in a
barred subject, which Lacan expresses with an ironic algorithm: S/s.
This formulation reflects an effort to reread Freud through Saussure's
structural linguistics and, less obviously but no less importantly, Lévi-
Strauss's structural anthropology.

The Lacanian subject (S/s) can be best understood in terms of the
structure of signification. Throughout his interrogation of the subject,
Lacan repeatedly asks: "Is the place that I occupy as the subject of a
signifier concentric or excentric, in relation to the place I occupy as the
subject of the signified?"[14] Every philosophy of self-consciousness, of
which Hegelianism is the paradigm, presupposes that the subject is
concentric. Lacan, however, is convinced that the subject is irreducibly
excentric and hence can never return to or be at home with itself.
"The radical heteronomy that Freud's discovery shows gaping within
man can never again be covered over without whatever is used to hide
it being profoundly dishonest."[15] In terms approaching religious testimony, Lacan explains:

> Kern unseres Wesen, the nucleus of our being, but it is not so much that
> Freud commands us to seek it as so many others before him have

with the empty adage 'Know thyself'—as to reconsider the ways that lead to it, and which he shows us. Or rather that which he proposes for us to attain is not that which can be the object of knowledge, but that (doesn't he tell us as much?) which creates our being and about which he teaches us that we bear witness to it as much and more in our whims, our aberrations, our phobias and fetishes, as in our more or less civilized personalities.[16]

From Lacan's perspective, "that which creates our being" is radically Other. This Other cannot be returned to the same. In contrast to Hegelian difference, which is always a moment in an all-encompassing identity, Lacanian difference cannot be reduced to identity.

Lacan is convinced that Freud's own texts warrant the use of structural linguistics. In *The Interpretation of Dreams*, Freud compares the dream to a "rebus" and suggests that the process of reading dreams is similar to the activity of translation:

> The dream-thought and the dream-content are presented to us like two versions of the same subject-matter in two different languages. Or, more properly, the dream-content seems like a transcript of the dream-thoughts into another mode of expression, whose characters and syntactic laws it is our business to discover by comparing the original and the translation. The dream-thoughts are immediately comprehensible, as soon as we have learnt them. The dream-content, on the other hand, is expressed as it were in a pictographic script, the characters of which have to be transposed individually into the language of the dream thoughts.[17]

The accounts of language developed by Saussure and Jakobson suggest a certain affinity between basic linguistic functions and the principles of dreamwork. The poetic practices of metaphor and metonomy describe the rules of substitution (condensation) and association (displacement) that govern linguistic activity and guide the formation of dreams. Combining the insights of Freud, Saussure, and Jakobson, Lacan argues that the unconscious is structured like a language. From this point of view, the subject appears to be a play of signification graphically depicted by complex elaborations of the basic formula S/s.

To appreciate the implications of Lacan's rewriting of Freudian psychology, it is necessary to understand precisely what he means by "language." Following Saussure, Lacan maintains that language is a differential structure of elements that are systematically combined according to laws so as to form a closed order of signification. It is important to stress that "language and its structure exist prior to the

moment at which each subject at a certain point in his mental development makes his entry into it."[18] Lacan expands his notion of ante-
cedent linguistic structure to include all the codes by which a culture
regulates the systems of exchange (for example, psychological, social,
political, economic) necessary for its own preservation. When understood in this broad sense, language stands for the entire symbolic order
and constitutes what Lacan describes as the Name of the Father. The
Name of the Father is the paternal law that bars the free expression
and full satisfaction of the subject's desire. In this sense, the Name of
the Father necessarily entails the refusal of the bar. Lacan's argument
turns on an innovative reinterpretation of Freud's "Copernican revolution," in which the unconscious decenters the self-conscious ego. The
creative subject does not constitute language or form the linguistic structures that guide human development. Rather, language constitutes the
subject and thus the subject is, in effect, a function of language. The
subject, in other words, is formed by the linguistic structures in and
through which it emerges.

Such formation is always incomplete. This incompletion suggests
that the refusal of the Lacanian bar must be understood in another
way. Not only does language refuse desire; desire also refuses language.
Desire, which, I have emphasized, can never be totally known or fully
expressed, escapes every effort to master it. In an effort to allow "the
Freudian thing" to "speak for itself," Lacan writes:

> . . . is it not enough to judge your defeat to see me [that is, the Freudian
> thing] escape first from the dungeon of the fortress in which you are so
> sure you have me secured by situating me not in you yourselves, but in
> being itself? I wander about in what you regard as being the least true in
> essence: in the dream, in the way the most far-fetched conceit, the most
> grotesque nonsense of the joke defies sense, in chance, not in its law,
> but in its contingency, and I never do more to change the face of the
> world than when I give it the profile of Cleopatra's nose.[19]

The unmasterable desire that "changes the face of the world" bars any
possibility of a transparent relation between signifier and signified (S/s).
In the absence of such transparency, the play of signification remains
endlessly obscure. This point must be underscored, for it is frequently
misunderstood. Lacan's claim that the unconscious is structured like a
language has led some of his interpreters to charge him with a form of
"logocentrism" in which consciousness can, in principle, be completely
deciphered.[20] A closer reading of Lacan's texts, however, discloses that
his notion of "language," in a manner not unlike Derrida's reading of
"writing," calls into question the possibility of such decipherability.

The endless obscurity of signification points to yet another dimension of the refusal of the bar. The bar itself refuses: the bar that both joins and separates signifier and signified (S/s) refuses representation. In the course of explaining the importance of Saussure's science of linguistics for psychoanalysis, Lacan argues that the "thematics of this science is henceforth suspended, in effect, at the primordial position of the signifier and the signified as being distinct orders separated initially by a barrier resisting signification. And that is what was to make possible an exact study of the connections proper to the signifier, and of the extent of their function in the genesis of the signified."[21] The condition of the possibility of signification is the *difference* between signifier and signified. This difference, which is graphed but not represented by a fine line, "/", "resists [or refuses] signification." Consequently, signification presupposes something in-significant. This insignificant "something" casts a shadow over the significance of every signification.

The refusals of the Lacanian bar make it impossible to re-fuse the subject. The subject is ever excentric. It is precisely this excentricity that the eccentricities of Lacan's styles—personal as well as writerly—seek to evoke and provoke. Forever divided, fissured, faulted, the subject never talks straight but always wears a mask. In a certain sense, Lacan's subject restores the relation between person and *persona*, the mask used by players in ancient drama. In (the) Lacanian play Oedipus remains barred from seeing himself face-to-face. Masks mask masks in a play that refuses to raise the curtain hanging before the inner world. Describing the transition from consciousness to self-consciousness, Hegel writes:

> The two extremes, the one, of the pure inner world, the other, that of the inner being gazing into this pure inner world, have now coincided, and just as they, *qua* extremes, have vanished, so too the mean, as something other than these extremes, has also vanished. This curtain hanging before the inner world is therefore drawn away, and we have the inner being [the 'I'] gazing into the inner world— the vision of the undifferentiated selfsame being, which repels itself from itself, posits itself as an inner being containing different moments, but for which equally these moments are immediately *not* different— *self-consciousness*.[22]

By rejecting the significance of Hegelian self-exposure, Lacan ventures the insignificance of Nietzschean play. This abyssal play is, as Derrida keeps telling us, a risky, though unavoidable, venture.

> The hermenuetic project that postulates a true meaning of the text is disqualified under this regime. Reading is freed from the horizon of

the meaning or truth of being, liberated from the values of the product's production or the presence of the present. . . . Truth in the guise of production, the unmasking/dissimulation of the present product, is dismantled [or, recalling our preoccupation with refuse, perhaps we might say 'is wasted'—with all the connotations that 'wasted' currently carries]. The veil [or curtain] is no more raised than it is lowered. Its suspense delimits—the epoch. To de-limit, to undo, to come undone, when it is a matter of the veil, does this not once again return to unveiling? Even to destroying a fetish? This question, *inasmuch as it is a question* . . . remains—interminably.[23]

A question remains—always remains—remains interminably. From the beginning, I have attempted to persist in questioning, to linger with questions. As I approach something like an end, one question in particular returns with a certain urgency: Do the death of God, the fading of the subject, and the end of the Law create the possibility of thinking what ontotheology has left unthought?

If the Law expresses the Name of the Father by repressing that which is never known, the unnameable Other might have something to do with Woman. This outlawed Woman would not be just any woman but would be the Woman that has been forgotten since the beginning of the "world." In a provocative essay entitled "God and the *Jouissance* of Woman: A Love Letter," Lacan suggests that this forgotten Woman "is" the goddess.[24]

Lacan imagines the creation of the world with the help of the Greeks.

[The creation of the world] required a *clinamen*,[25] an inclination, at some point. When Democritus tried to designate it, presenting himself as already the adversary of a pure function of negativity in order to introduce thought into it, he says, *It is not the meden that is essential*, and adds—thus showing you that from what one of my pupils called the archaic stage of philosophy, the manipulation of words was used as in the time of Heidegger—*it is not a meden, but a den*, which, in Greek, is a coined word. He did not say *en* let alone *on*. What, then, did he say? He said, answering the question I asked today, of idealism, *Nothing, perhaps?*— not *perhaps nothing*, but *not nothing* [Rien, peut-être? non pas—peut-être rien, mais pas rien].[26]

Following Heidegger, Lacan establishes a link between the Latin *res* and the French *rien*. Heidegger underscores the relation between *res*, which is associated with *rien*, and *causa*, which eventually develops into the Romance *la cosa* and finally appears as the French *la chose*.

Res . . . rien . . . causa . . . chose. This thing that is no-thing seems to be
the cause of everything.

But what is a cause? There is no easy answer to this question, for,
as Lacan stresses, a cause is a "hole" (*trou*), or "gap" (*gap*), which has
"the character of an absolute point without any knowledge."[28]

> Whenever we speak of a cause . . . there is always something anti-
> conceptual, something indefinite. The phases of the moon are the
> causes of tides—we know this from experience, we know that the
> word cause is correctly used here. Or again, miasmas are the cause of
> fever—that doesn't mean anything either, there is a hole, and some-
> thing that oscillates in the interval. In short, there is a cause only in
> something that doesn't work [*qui cloche*].[29]

Within a Lacanian economy, that which doesn't work always points to
(which is not to say represents) the unconscious. The interval of the
indefinite notion 'cause' makes the opening of the unconscious. "This
indicates that the cause of the unconscious—and you see that the word
cause [like the word of] is to be taken here in its ambiguity, a cause to
be sustained, but also a function of the cause at the level of the
unconscious—this cause must be conceived fundamentally as a lost
cause [*une cause perdue*]."[30]

The Lacanian "lost cause" is even more ambiguous than is usually
realized. In a claim that most of his interpreters would prefer to forget
or repress, Lacan notes an unexpected dimension of his exploration
of the unconscious: "I am speaking of religion in the true sense of the
term—not of a desiccated, methodologized religion, repressed into the
distant past of a primitive thought, but of religion as we see it practised
in a still living, very vital way."[31] Elsewhere Lacan confesses: "For the
myth of the *God is dead*—which, personally, I feel much less sure about,
as a myth of course, than most contemporary intellectuals, which is in
no sense a declaration of theism, nor of faith in the resurrection—
perhaps, this myth is simply a shelter against the threat of castration."[32]
As Lacan emphasizes, his resistance to the myth of the death of God in
no way involves a return to traditional religious belief. Lacan's mispri-
sion of Freud points toward a genuine "atheism" that approximates
what Bataille labels "atheology." "For the true formula of atheism is not
God is dead—even by basing the origin of the function of the father
upon his murder, Freud protects the father—the true formula of atheism is *God is unconscious*."[33] The unconscious that is "God" is, for Lacan,
eternally feminine. When considering Lacan's rereading of Freud, it is
always important to remember his insistence that what leads Freud
on, in his relentless chase, is "his passion for the goddess."[34]

To approach the goddess, one must refuse the refusal of the bar. Such refusal is always transgressive. The space of transgression is created by bars that open, if ever, only at night.

> Contemplating night, I see nothing, love nothing. I remain immobile, frozen, absorbed in IT [*ELLE*]. I can imagine a landscape of terror, sublime, the earth open as a volcano, the sky filled with fire, or any other vision capable of "ravishing" the spirit; as beautiful and disturbing as it may be, night surpasses this limited "possible" and yet IT is nothing [*ELLE n'est rien*], there is nothing sensible in IT, not even finally darkness. In IT, everything fades away, but, exorbitant, I traverse an empty depth and the empty depth traverses me. In IT, I communicate with the "unknown" opposed to the *ipse* that I am; I become *ipse*, unknown to myself, two terms confounded in a single rending, hardly differing from a void — not able to be distinguished from it by anything that I can grasp — nevertheless differing from it more than does the world of a thousand colors.[35]

Notes

1. Thomas J. J. Altizer, *The Descent into Hell: A Study of the Radical Reversal of the Christian Consciousness* (New York: Seabury Press, 1979), 150-51.

2. G.W.F. Hegel, *The Philosophy of History*, trans. J. Sibree (New York: Dover Publications, 1956), 103.

3. Ibid., 316-17.

4. Ibid., 324.

5. G.W.F. Hegel, *Phenomenology of Spirit*, trans. A.V. Miller (New York: Oxford University Press, 1977), 14.

6. Ibid., 14.

7. Jacques Derrida, *Positions*, trans. Alan Bass (Chicago: University of Chicago Press, 1981), 77-78.

8. See: Alexandre Kojève, *Introduction à la lecture de Hegel: Leçons sur la Phénoménologie de l'Esprit professées de 1933 à 1939 à l'Ecole des Hautes Etudes* (Paris: Gallimard, 1947).

9. Maurice Merleau-Ponty, *Sens et non-sens* (Paris: Nagel, 1948), 109-10.

10. Jacques Lacan, *Ecrits*, trans. Alan Sheridan (New York: W. W. Norton, 1977), 166.

11. Hegel, *Phenomenology of Spirit*, 486.

12. Lacan, *Ecrits*, 2.

13. Ibid., 1.

14. Ibid., 165.

15. Ibid., 172.

16. Ibid., 173-74.

17. Sigmund Freud, *The Interpretation of Dreams*, trans. J. Strachey (New York: Avon Books, 1965), 311-12.

18. Ibid., 148.

19. Ibid., 122.

20. At one point, Derrida seems to read Lacan in this way. See: "Freud and the Scene of Writing," in *Writing and Difference*, trans. A. Bass (Chicago: University of Chicago Press, 1978), 169-231.

21. Lacan, *Ecrits, op. cit.*, 149.

22. Hegel, *Phenomenology of Spirit, op. cit.*, 103.

23. Jacques Derrida, *Spurs: Nietzsche's Styles*, trans. B. Harlow (Chicago: University of Chicago Press, 1978), 107, 109.

24. Jacques Lacan, *Feminine Sexuality: Jacques Lacan and the école freudienne*, ed. J. Mitchell and J. Rose, trans. J. Rose (New York: W. W. Norton, 1982).

25. *Clinamen* derives from the Latin, *clinare*, to incline. For a rich exploration of this complex notion, see Harold Bloom, *Poetry and Repression: Revisionism from Blake to Stevens* (New Haven: Yale University Press, 1976). For Bloom's account of the theological implications of this notion, see *Kabbalah and Criticism* (New York: Seabury Press, 1975).

26. Jacques Lacan, *The Four Fundamental Concepts of Psychoanalysis*, ed. Jacques-Alain Miller, trans. A. Sheridan (New York: W. W. Norton, 1981), 63-64.

27. Martin Heidegger, "The Thing," *Poetry, Language, Thought*, trans. A. Hofstadter (New York: Harper and Row, 1971), 175-76.

28. Lacan, *The Four Fundamental Concepts of Psychoanalysis*, 22, 253.

29. Ibid., 22.

30. Ibid., 128.

31. Ibid., 7.

32. Ibid., 27.

33. Ibid., 59.

34. Lacan, *Ecrits*, 124.

35. Georges Bataille, *L'Expérience intérieure* (Paris: Gallimard, 1954), 145.

Works Cited

Altizer, Thomas J.J. *The Descent into Hell: A Study of the Radical Reversal of Christian Consciousness*. New York: Seabury Press, 1979.

Bataille, Georges. *L'Experience interieure*. (Paris: Gallimard, 1954.

Derrida, Jacques. "Freud and the Scene of Writing." In *Writing and Difference*. Trans. Alan Bass. Chicago: University of Chicago Press, 1978.

_____. *Positions*. Trans. Alan Bass. Chicago: University of Chicago Press, 1981.

Freud, Sigmund. *The Interpretation of Dreams*. Trans. J. Strachey. New York: Avon Books, 1965.

_____. *Spurs: Nietzsche's Styles*. Trans. B. Harlow. Chicago: University of Chicago Press, 1978.

Hegel, G.W.F. *The Phenomenology of Spirit*. Trans. A. V. Miller. New York: Oxford University Press, 1977.

_____. *The Philosophy of History* Trans. J. Sibree. New York: Dover Publications, 1956.

Heidegger, Martin. "The Thing." In *Poetry, Language, Thought*. Trans. A. Hofstadter. New York: Harper and Row, 1971.

Kojève, Alexandre. *Introduction à la lecture de Hegel; Leçons sur la Phénoménologie de L'Esprit professées de 1933 a 1939 à L'Ecole des Hautes Etudes*. Paris: Gallimard, 1947.

Lacan, *Ecrits.* Trans. Alan Sheridan (New York: W. W. Norton, 1977.

_____. *The Four Fundamental Concepts of Psychoanalysis.* Ed. Jacques-Alain Miller, trans. Alan Sheridan. New York: W. W. Norton, 1981.

Merleau-Ponty, Maurice. *Sens et non-sens.* Paris: Nagel, 1948.

Mitchell, J. and J. Rose, eds. *Feminine Sexuality: Jacques Lacan and the école freudienne.* New York: W.W. Norton and Company, 1982.

Summary

David Crownfield

Mark Taylor raises a number of interesting issues, relating the law, the subject, and the linguistic bar to the questions of Lacan and theological discourse.

Taylor situates the traditional concept of the Law in the context of the relation between a transcendent God and an autonomous self. After the death of God, the institution of the Law must be reexamined. Such a reexamination can be sited in the context of Lacan's subversive rereading of Hegel. For Hegel, Spirit posits itself as other, and returns to itself from the other, ultimately sublating all otherness, mastering all difference, in pure self-consciousness. Lacan judges that this whole project is impossible, because the unconscious is irreducible and precludes the absolute self-transparency of consciousness.

But once the subject is disidentified from consciousness, who is this "I"? It cannot be, with Hegel (or even with Sartre), pure being-for-itself. The notion of "I" as a perduring integrated ego is a specular image, a fictional unity always irreducible and discordant with respect to the living reality. Desire, for Hegel, can be satisfied when the subject is at home with itself in being other; for Lacan, it can never be satisfied: it is the marker of this irreducible discord in the heart of the subject. The subject of the signifier and the subject of the signified are not concentric. And difference here, in contrast with Hegel, cannot be sublated into identity, but remains split.

Language, including the whole ensemble of structures of social codes, the entire symbolic order, is for such an excentric subject a pregiven law into which each subject at a particular point of development makes her entry. This pregiven law, the "Name-of-the-Father," bars the free expression and full satisfaction of the subject's desires. This is accomplished in part by the fact that language constitutes the subject, incomplete, decentered, without words for its desire. Taylor speaks of this as "unmasterable" desire, which bars any transparent relation between signifier and signified. Signification thus remains endlessly obscure, permanently undecipherable. (I am not convinced that this is correct; Taylor, like Winquist, seems to me to hold to a residual romanticism of desire that has been radically deconstructed by Lacan.)

Not just the content of the language, but the very bar of connection and separation between signifier and signified prevents the achievement of signification: this difference between signifier and signified itself cannot be signified, cannot be made itself to signify, and thus subverts the significance of every signification. The subject that has entered into such a language is ever excentric, ever divided, masked. Taylor reminds us of Derrida's recognition that this precludes any notion of *the* meaning of the text. Language as law, law as language, constitute and decenter, purport to name but perpetually veil, the subject, the real, the Other.

Taylor aims toward a conclusion by asking whether the death of God, the fading of the subject, the end of the Law, create the possibility of thinking what ontotheology has left unthought. The Law, as Name of the Father, represses that which is never known, the unnameable Other, which might have something to do with Woman—an outlawed, forgotten "the" woman, that has been forgotten since the beginning of the world. He reads Lacan's provocative essay on "God and the Jouissance of [sic!] Woman" as suggesting that "this forgotten Woman is the goddess." But Lacan says, [in *Feminine Sexuality*, 144] "There is no such thing as *the* woman, where the definite article stands for the universal."

For Taylor, the unsaid, the Other, the Woman, the goddess forgotten since the beginning, bears on the creation, is perhaps the cause of everything. A cause, he quotes Lacan, is a hole, a gap, an absolute point without any knowledge. "There is a cause only where there is something that doesn't work"—the unconscious, a lost cause. Lacan remarked that the true formula of atheism is "God is unconscious." Taylor observes, "The unconscious that is 'God' is, for Lacan, eternally feminine." Lacan, he says, insisted that "what leads Freud on, in his relentless chase, is 'his passion for the goddess.' " (In the complex text in which this image is embedded, in which Lacan locates Freud in the myth of Actaeon and Diana, Freud's pursuit is a quest for truth that leads to the issue of death.)

In conclusion Taylor says that, to approach the goddess, one must refuse and transgress the refusal of the bar (the repression of desire?).

Taylor's treatment of the barred, decentered, divided subject, and the consequent deconstruction of traditional views of law, of language, of meaning, is useful, especially as it is brought to focus in the juxtaposition of Lacan with Hegel. He recognizes the importance of the Law of the Father for the barring of desire, the splitting of the subject, the access to language. He helps us see the relations between Lacan's and Derrida's critiques of subject and of meaning: Derrida's *différance* as differing, differentiating, deferring takes the place of the Hegelian self-consciousness with its self-objectification and self-reunion, in the substitutions, displacements, deferrals, in which desire plays through language.

There are, however, two or three points on which I want to raise questions about Taylor's reading of Lacan, which bear directly on the question of theological discourse. Taylor contends that the absence of transparency of the signifier to a signified entails an "endless obscurity of signification." This obscurity is a function of "unmasterable desire." He says, correctly, that for Lacan, desire is never satisfied; but he refers back to this point later in the words, "Since desire cannot be totally satisfied . . ." But the problem is not that the satisfaction of desire is incomplete, and it is not that desire is an unmasterable power. The problem, according to Lacan, is that desire is inherently illusory, an artifact of the barring of the subject, the splitting of the self. It is not a force to be mastered but an inescapable illusion to be (partially) disarmed by its entry into language, into the domain of symbolic discourse. The consequence is that, in every signification, desire is always deferred, dislocated down through the discourse from signifier to signifier without finding its Other. But this does not mean the obscurity of signification, in the symbolic domain of public discourse, but only an irreducible dichotomy between its public, symbolic functions and its unattainable imaginary function to present the Other.

The second point at issue has to do with the notion of refusing the refusal of the bar. I take it that this means to adopt a transgressive style of thinking (and acting) that is not blocked by the Law from pursuing its passion for the goddess, the Other as primordial Woman, the "night" of the Bataille quotation that ends the essay. But this unattainable pursuit is just what, according to Lacan, brings the analysand to the analyst: the refusal to renounce the quest for Mother, to accept the Law of the Father, to submit to the displacements and substitutions that constitute the language, and enter into the world of the symbolic.

Theology, for Taylor, seems to be in a sense a discourse situated in conscious defiance of the father, in the pursuit of Mother in eroticized discourse, in the illusion that desire, even though unattainable, is the truth rather than the lie of our existence. His evocations of the delights and passions of transgression are immensely appealing, and as an analogue of the psychoanalytic process of bringing desire into speech they resonate powerfully with the issues Lacan is dealing with. But, so far as the concepts in this essay are concerned, and so far as I have rightly understood what he is saying, Taylor has located theology in an eroticism of impossible desire rather than of occasional enjoyment (*jouissance*), in the imaginary rather than in the symbolic. This is where Freud locates religion in *The Future of an Illusion,* but it is not clear to me whether it is what Taylor intends.

3.

Jacques Lacan and the Magic of Desire: A Post-Structuralist Subscript

Carl Raschke

> Tell me, enigmatical man, whom do you love best,
> your father, your mother, your sister or your brother?
>
> > I have neither father, nor mother, nor sister, nor
> > brother.
> > Your friends?
> > Now you use a word whose meaning I have never
> > known.
> > Your country?
> > I do not know in what latitude it lies.
> > Beauty?
> > I could indeed love her, Goddess and Immortal.
> > Gold?
> > I hate it as you hate God.
> > Then, what do you love. extraordinary stranger?
> > I love the clouds . . . the clouds that pass . . . up
> > there . . . up there . . . the wonderful clouds!
> > > —Charles Baudelaire, *Paris Spleen*

"What we have learned from Saussure," Merleau-Ponty has written, "is that, taken singly, signs do not signify anything, and that each one of them does not so much express a meaning as mark a divergence of meaning between itself and other signs."[1] The age of Lacan commences with the death of the signified. It is perhaps what we really have in mind when we prate about the "post-modern."[2] The morning star of modernism, of course, has always been the Cartesian *cogito*, the interiorization of the previous two millenia of metaphysical thought which at last resulted in the summation and closure of the book of Christian theology. From the advent of Cartesian "speculation," the discovery of *speculatio* or "self-mirroring," the moment of transcendental reflexivity, springs the passion of modern inquiry and modern criticism. Modernity has enshrined the power of the sign in the same way that postmodernism has applied the didactical strategy of *difference*. The power of the sign derives from the projection toward the infinite of an historically constituted literacy, and by extension a textuality, which has been severed from any "natural" systematics of reflection and representations, as Foucault has described it.[3] The epoch of the sign coincides with the ideology of the "human," the immortalizing of the collective capacity for self-representation, so that classic epistemology is inverted as psychology. Yet the psychology of the modern can only stray so far. The operation of the sign as a deracinated style of apostolic authority, as a post-Medieval simulacrum for heavenly charisma, degrades into the existentialist pathos of defiance, the *Wille zur Macht* of Romantic subjectivism.

It is here amidst a culture where the Cartesian *cogito* has become in effect an "image of the beast," a duplicate of the divine, a virtual apparition of the transcendental signified, that Lacan's metacriticism from the "psychological" standpoint gains credence. Modernity has "postulated" the subject in much the same fashion that the Kantian architectonic of reason was compelled to postulate the Deity. The subject must both inhere and subsist, or so Descartes realized, as a stolid requirement of philosophical argument and construction. It is the Archimedean point at which the entire structure of what we might call the "discourse of experiment" is balanced and held intact. In the modern idiom the Cartesian subject operates as the unifying principle of all inference and conceptual innovation. This necessity was grasped immediately by German idealism, and it soon became the founding insight for Hegel's reconstitution of "science" as a dialectical synthesis of thinking and experience. Yet Lacan's premise serves to subvert the subject's metaphysical suzerainty at its very own hallowed site. The "deconstruction" of the subject in the Lacanian mode arises from the revelation that subjectivity itself is not an "object" that all speech denotes, but an *introjective* consequence of the mimetic structure of language itself. As Lacan notes, "the subject is subject only from being subjected to the field of the Other."[4] The power that the Other enjoys to define and configure knowledge through wielding syntactical regularities rebounds upon the formation of all "self-conscious" representations, and thus creates the subject as God authors the world.

At the same time, the unmasking of the subject is its primordial *disclosure*, the removal of the reification, or *closure*, of the interplay of signifiers within the space of cognition. The disclosure of the subject is the unrestraining of the energy of desire. Again, in Lacan's delphic formulation:

> The truth, in this sense, is that which runs after truth—and that is where I am running, where I am taking you, like Actaeon's hounds, after me. When I find the goddess's hiding place, I will no doubt be changed into a stag, and you can devour me. . . . [5]

The location of the subject in the "goddess's" lair betokens a kind of primitive reunion between the discourse of the Other and the moment in which the subject is formed from what Lacan terms "the deconstruction of the drive." The language of the analyst in this sense performs as the hermetic trickster, luring the client toward the abyss of self-revelation where the mediations or "constructions" of the analysand dissolve into the enchantments of the "it" (Freud's *id*). The liminal representations of "subjectivity" at this point emerge as the charter language of the hidden "constitution" for multiple modes of discourse posing as a weave of signifiers. The act of signification springs out of what we might term the "dark intentionality" of desire itself, although the very *logos* of desire, a silent erotology, cannot be deciphered alone, but must be read as a companion volume to the virtual structure of meaning and presence that constitutes the "logic" of the text. The syntactics of the "soul," the so-called "humanities," thus are built upon this dark intentionality. As Hamann first glimpsed and Freud later detailed through the methodology of regression, the protostructure of conversation is myth. Myth itself, as Levi-Strauss has discerned, turns upon the logic of opposition. But the opposition is not a social contradiction or a cognitive conundrum. The Oedipus myth, for instance, is not primarily a struggle against the belief in autochthony. Instead it can be comprehended as a mimetic response to the lesion of "consciousness" etched by the inauguration of discourse. The Lacanian *Spaltung*, "the split . . . which the subject undergoes by virtue of being a subject only in so far as he speaks,"[6] stands forth as the scene of primal repression and as the power of *re-presentation*.

Here language commences, not as a ludic exercise in symbol-manufacture, but as a veritable division of the darkness, a groping toward functional clarity in contest with the restiveness of unarticulated desire. The Lacanian framework of language, viewed primordially and hence poststructurally, is the same as the Heraclitean *logos*, which has always been expressed mythically. It is γιϑ νομξνων ϑφρ πϛντων κϛτϛ τδν λσϑον τσυδξ, that originary production of measured strife or counterpoint which resides in "psyche," which forever presses into the light of day, yet remains "strange" to those who seek to discern its working.[7] The "truth" of Heraclitus lingers in singular obscurity; it is recovered through the exposure of the duplicity of the phenomenal, corresponding in psychological terms to the saying of the archetypically unsaid, the step backwards into what remains prior to the chain of signification. The "splitting" of desire is tantamount to the founding of the unconscious, which is not so much a topology as a reverse projection, a projection of discourse which remains charged with the numinosity of its own overwhelming self-presence. The carnival of representation perpetrated through the historicizing and codifying of discourse must ultimately be summarized as the deflection of the drive into language.

Language is the palingenesis of desire. Structuralism all along has assumed, falsely, that it is a "parthenogenesis." But this palingenesis, which transpires amid the agitation of writing and the elaboration of textual markers, is subject to its own de-constitution, its *analysis* in the strict sense. The ages of discourse are a kind of yellow-brick road wending toward the site of disenchantment. The disenchantment of discourse comes with the discovery that *each signification is a mystification*, that the production of referents is but high magic.

The alleged "structure" of the unconscious, therefore, is commensurate with a magical semantics. But what do we mean by "magic?" The field of the magical, and by extension its intricate pathology, has been a cause of avoidance not only for philosophy and theology, but for just about all orthodox modes of hermeneutical investigation. The category of the magical does not belong within its organon of inference. Why not? Because whatever is "magic" presupposes a secrecy that by definition cannot be either contemplated or made a predicate. Its occultation suffices as its primacy, as its power. The secret force of the magical subject distends the chain of signifiers. The magical subject, which constitutes the subject *in terminis*, is the discursive instrumentality of desire. What in Freud's mechanico-metaphysical schema of pushes and pulls has been known, quite tendentiously, as "cathexis" is changed through the Lacanian series of conceptual transgressions into the discontinuity of the wish. Lacan understands, of course, that Freud's so-called "hydraulics" of the unconscious was but an expansive metaphor for the displacement of desire in the direction of a disguised *desideratum*. Lacan notes that in the parapraxis, in the riddle of dream life, in the myth, hovers "the sense of impediment." The impediment is not a task, but a secret mode of signification, what Derrida has called the "supplement." The infrastructure of the text is not revealed by the linkage of signifiers, but by their unraveling and erasure. Repression both hides and unveils simultaneously.

Thus analysis comprises a return to the scene not where the subject is to be found, but where it was *perpetrated*. The subject has been perpetrated in the breach, the breach imparted by desire. The illumination of the unconscious shows nothing, for the unconscious is not to be found. "We have," says Lacan, "in Eurydice twice lost, the most potent image we can find of the relation between Orpheus the analyst and the unconscious."[8] Eurydice is a magical entity, because she exists as an erotic phosphorescence, as pure heterogeneity, as a representation that flickers forth from the ancient division of names. She is "metonymic," as Lacan would argue. In other words, the "meaning" of the unconscious is the strategy of self-concealment. The language of the unconscious is the language of feints, diversions, and masks. It is the vocabulary of the magus.

The psychology of magic, as contrasted with its semantics, depends on the harboring, through anticipation rather than enunciation, of the forgotten name of the "god." A calculated confession of the workings of this psychology can be found in the writings of Aleister Crowley, the notorious *Meistersinger* for the magical theater of the twentieth century. It is incumbent upon the magician, Crowley tells us, to seek the "Lost Word," whose "pronunciation is synonymous with the accomplishment of the Great Work."[9] The "lost word," the *logos* that does not speak, is the supreme magical cipher, because its power seeps from its very inarticulation. The great work, the *magnum opus*, the transformation of the inchoate into a vast, intelligible content, turns upon the saying of the aboriginal unsaid, the presyntactic. "An idea is perpetuated because it must never be mentioned."[10] The refusal to speak, the veiling of what remains so difficult to utter, defines the magician's hegemony within the court of symbols. The magician controls the energy of the god because he "knows" it as the mystery of the cleft, as the message of the vestige, as the manifestation of the trace. Indeed, the magician is greater than the god, insofar as he reserves the prerogative of commanding what wavers in the darkness of the unimagined into the realm of voice. Magic requires both silence and renunciation.

The preference of the magician for the prediscursive perhaps helps us understand one of the long-persisting curiosities in the history of philosophy — Plato's disdain for the use of writing. Writing is amnesia, according to Plato. Plato recounts the king of Egypt's rebuttal to Theuth, inventor of the graphic and computative skills, who vows that writing will improve the art of memory. But the king protests: "If men learn this, it will implant forgetfulness in their souls; they will cease to exercise memory because they rely on that which is written, calling things to remembrance no longer from within themselves, but by means of external marks."[11] The king, whose views are also Plato's, fears writing as a kind of artifice, a magical substitute for authentic recollection. The king well understands that writing involves repression, that the resort to a mnemonic technology of signs and codes must lead to the uncoupling of meaning from its source along with the creation of a metaphoric web of dissemblances. Plato's own metaphysics of representation was in many ways a sentimental gesture toward retrieving the arcana of the soul that have been left disinherited by the rise of philosophical argument. Socrates himself laments several lines later about the perfidy of "written words":

> . . . they seem to talk to you as though they were intelligent, but if you ask them anything about what they say, from a desire to be instructed, they go on telling you just the same thing forever. And once a thing is put in writing, the composition, whatever it may be, drifts all over the place, getting into the hands not only of those who understand it, but equally of those who have no business with it; it doesn't know how to address the right people, and not address the wrong. And when it is ill-treated and unfairly abused it always needs its parent to come to its help.[12]

Writing results, as Derrida has told us, in the erasure of presence and the dissemination of significance through the temporality of the text. But this erasure, which amounts to a repression of the "face" (*eidos*) of the original "divinity," produces a force or tension that is now distributed throughout the whole genealogy of the text. The lattice of signifiers is anchored not in a founding signification, but in the contretemps of forgetfulness.

The first inscription, or protowriting, is therefore a mode of magical pseudomemory. It consists of what the ancients termed *hierogrammatica* ("hieroglyphs"), a picture-script that evokes by representation the sense of what is hidden, or forbidden. The hieroglyph eventually becomes the model for the hermetic cosmology of magical correspondences, which was employed as an aid to memory in classical rhetoric. The rules of memory, evoking magical images of things invisible, were indispensible to the art of truth-speaking and persuading an audience to the truth.[13] From the psychoanalytic perspective, we may say that the theory of magical correspondences as the *pretext* of discourse mirrors the relationship between desire and representation, between meaning and metonymy. Magic is not an aberration of reason so much as it constitutes an intermediate "logic" between the formations of the unconscious and the discipline of expression, which depends upon the "grammatology" endemic to all linguistic architectures. Magic flourishes when words are not allowed entirely to have their say. Magic is the effort to build a system of manipulable representations during the twilight hour when the "god" has vanished and his absence has not yet been consecrated as discourse.

The magical, therefore, comprises the misplaced signifier that the sort of structuralism Lacan has borrowed from Saussure can entirely assimilate. The magical is less than what Lacan terms the "symbolic"; it is certainly something more than the "imaginary." The magical is the *logos* that makes possible the "return of the repressed." In Lacan's words, it is the plan of investigation that fortifies the subject "in his encounter with the filth that may support him." Whereas the goal of Platonic *anamnesis* was self-purification, the outcome of Lacanian regression is to generate a countertext to the perjured testimony of the *cogito*. This countertext becomes its own argot. Lacan writes:

> Take Socrates. The inflexible purity of Socrates and his *atopia* are correlative. Intervening, at every moment, there is the demonic voice.[14]

Psychoanalysis acts as the scribe for this countertext, the "demonic voice" of the subject who is constrained to speak of his passion, but can only disclose its intention through the supplementarity that characterizes the stitch of signifiers. The Socratic demon is not the augur, but the taunt of philosophy. The demon is the "it" that holds forth, that converses in a strange way, as what Lacan terms a "colophon" to the Cartesian meditation, to the discourse of subjectivity. The colophon, however, belongs to the text in the sense that it simultaneously marks and deciphers it. "I" and "it" are coimplicative. The magician tends to the vocalization of that which is unintelligible within the idiom of the subject. The magician possesses the "lost word," the revelation of desire which paradoxically can never be laid bare, because it is the shade of the Other, the shudder of the real. The Freudian project was to eliminate the illusion of a magic world through the disclosure of desire. The Lacanian enterprise is to show that desire cannot be disclosed, because it is the root of language, the thing in itself, the loom behind the weave of signifiers. For "desire is that which is manifested in the interval that demands within itself, in as much as the subject, in articulating the signifying chain, brings to light the want-to-be, together with the appeal to receive the complement from the Other, if the Other, the locus of speech, is also the locus of this want, or lack."[15] Because in Lacanian linguistics the signifier ultimately signifies nothing, the world of representation can be construed as the ritualization of magic. And magic conjures up a sense of presence where, in actuality, there is only the *repressed*.

The psychic mechanism of the surrogate presence was first examined in a brief essay of Freud's titled "The 'Uncanny,'" written in 1919. Freud's speculations, while maddeningly tentative and a bit too casual, do indicate the fruitful hermeneutical possibilities inherent in the psychoanalytic method, once leave has been taken from its more "dogmatic" strictures. Freud sets about to examine the meaning of the expression *unheimlich* ("uncanny" or "unfamiliar") as it pertains to the feeling of the supernatural or haunted, particularly as conveyed in horror literature. Freud asks what is truly signified by the fictive construct of the "alien" presence. The mood of uncanniness is inextricably bound up with the phenomenon of repression, according to Freud. But it is not due simply to repression of the specific wish-object. The uncanny arises when an entire psychic range of orientation—primary narcissism, for instance, which first found cultural legitimacy in primitive, animistic thought formations—invades the ego system, disrupting its capacity for critical discrimination. "An uncanny effect," Freud observes, "is often and easily produced by effacing the distinction between imagination and reality, such as ... when a symbol takes over the full functions and significance of the thing it symbolizes. ... It is this element which contributes not a little to the uncanny effect attaching to magical practices."[16] The domination of the object by the symbol, or more precisely the token by the force of desire, depends on a superimposition of significatory complexes, or grammars. The uncanny emerges with the unthrottling of discursive operations or, in Lacan's terms, with the "splitting" of the subject from its innermost self, the production of the subject through independent, symbolical activity. Whereas Freud understood the uncanny as the atavism of some discarded habit of cognition, the Lacanian view permits us to regard it as the penumbra of self-discursiveness. The uncanny is the revelation of the "unconscious" as a totalized sector of discourse, as a conjugate semantics to the "rational" order of both personal and cultural reflection.

The uncanny is "strange," or "not at home," because it represents the magical presence of a mobile desire which cannot settle down in ordinary language. The uncanny is the reminder not merely of the "unconscious" in its antediluvian mystery, but of the very *arche-language* that is not language in the formal sense, but makes language possible. The Lacanian deconstruction of the totalized logic of significatory systems, therefore, aims at a new kind of postmodern transcendentalism. It is neither the transcendental metaphysics of Kant nor the illuminist subjectivism of the Romantics. It is a provisional sort of poststructuralist transcendentalism, an exceptionally incisive *via negativa* that pursues (in Derrida's wording) the "archaeology of the frivolous." The frivolous, in this instance, is the inessential, the wholly sensible or phenomenal, the myriad modalities of chatter. The discourse of the uncanny is the "structure" of magic.

The category of magic in this respect helps us to comprehend what structuralist thought has mistakenly interpreted as the eternal, *transformational* agency of the "unconscious." For example, in Levi-Strauss the unconscious operates as a timeless source of representational patterns that supplies the "mythic" format for narrative, ritual, and individual experience. The "vocabulary" of the imaginative performance, argues Levi-Strauss, "matters less than the structure," which is "atemporal" and "limited in its laws."[17] In typical Kantian fashion, Levi-Strauss stresses the genesis of symbol-configurations from an aprioristic universal mind. But while structuralism has grasped what might be called the "*transpersonal*" dimensions of mythico-symbolical reflection in relation to the empirical grammars of culture and language, it has failed to develop a useful account of the alleged semantic conversions that take place in the transition from the deeper unconscious to social cognition. The evident shortcomings of the structuralist program at this level ought best to be explained as a telltale flaw in the methodology itself. Only when the supposed structural transformations have been "destructured" in the measure that they now function as transpositional keys, rather than as underlying registers of meaning, can many apparent "solutions" to the enigma of human creativity be carried out. The transpositions between regular discourse and the subtext of the "unconscious" can now be seen as relative shifts in interpretation, not as perennial and inviolable norms.

Both structural anthropology and analytical psychology in the twentieth century have stoked the illusion that somehow the puzzles of the "irrational" could be described as a sophisticated kind of encrypting, which a proper metaphysics of the imagination might dispel. Even the more recent discovery of the primacy of desire, so far as it undercuts the ideological posturings of every formal hermeneutics, has been bent toward reestablishing the structuralist *myth of myths*. The allusion here, of course, is to the work of Jameson, who seeks to introduce the (Marxian) construct of social mediation as the horizon of both the historical and the textual, as a curious strategy of co-optation for the philosophical moment in which signification is deconstituted as writing, or *écriture*. Marxism, for Jameson, permits not simply a fundamental interpretation of synchronous codes according to certain "naturalistic" processes embedded in collective symbol-making but more importantly the retelling of history, a vaster narrative that unfolds "within the unity of a single great collective story."[18] Can the concept of social mediation suffice for the rule of "difference" in the deconstruction of textual artifacts? No. Jameson merely dusts off the metalanguage of structuralist semiotics and gives it a somewhat chic, Marxist polish. But the substance of the two hermeneutical approaches is identical. Jameson substitutes for Levi-Strauss's keyword "myth" the semanteme known as "history." History is transmuted from cultural text to social narrative. The dominion of desire is now pacified in a strange, convoluted "*ideo-*

logical" move as "the experience of Necessity," which Jameson insists must forestall the reification of historical interpretation. Jameson remarks that "history is what hurts, it is what refuses desire and sets inexorable limits to individual as well as collective praxis." That is "indeed the ultimate sense in which history as ground and untranscendable horizon needs no particular theoretical justification."[19]

In a very odd manner Jameson himself actually exposes both the conceit, and the deceit, of the Marxist valorization of time. For desire is unconditionally bounded, and therefore nullified, by a perverse kind of *ananke*, which Jameson claims as a principle of transcendence. Marxian transcendence is actually the closure of history, the qualification of desire in terms of the *puissance* of the collective, the sham deconstruction of the ideological scaffolding of interpretation only for the sake of a final totalization, or reification, of culture—the "great beast," *the human*. Marxism thus elaborates its own code of magic. Despite Jameson's critique of what he terms the "magical narratives" of the modern epoch enforced by a bourgeois schizophrenia afflicting both symbols and work, Marxism retains its own magical syntax. Jameson comes close to making such an admission when he talks about the requirement to "rewrite certain religious concepts," including "the pretheological systems of primitive magic" as "anticipatory foreshadowings of historical materialism."[20] The magical codings of Marxist rhetoric and analysis are exhibited in its readings of the revolution as, to borrow Jameson's phraseology, "utopian" consummations of the dominion of desire. In the would-be consummation lies the great "construction," or history as representation, which robs the function of desire of its dissimulative task. Social mediation, or the megaform of "society" itself, is not only the glyph for the unriddling of Marxian "theology," it also becomes the sounding device for its dark history. The dominion of desire can never be a metaphor for the human collective. It can only serve as the shadow of the utopian presumption, as a torment, like Ozymandias's mocking inscription, to the structuralist ideality.

In consequence, the Lacanian analytic rushes in where Marxian metahistory fears to tread. The Lacanian analytic understands desire as the truly unreifiable, not the sign of signs, but the moving *signature*. From desire the sanctuary of intelligibility is first built, and then torn down. As Lacan puts it, "*desidero* is the Freudian *cogito*."[21] Desire is kindled alongside the discourse of the Other; it is the precise momentum of the charged reflex called "consciousness" that spins about the axes of subjectivity and alterity. If we take Lacan quite seriously, we understand far more than the "metonymic" truth that the recital of his name enters into the history of thought a *lacune*, a hiatus, a "desideratum." We understand that the utterance of the *nom de père*, the "Name of the Father," is an accession to the founding, "deconstructive" moment when Oedipus has at last been banished, when the totalizing magic of the unconscious and all its narcissistic, romantic, and utopian fugues of overdetermined instinctuality have been obliterated in the judgment of language. The Lacanian lacuna, therefore, is the great crack in the ramparts of late modernism. It is the demystification of the demystifiers. It is truly the "end" of ideology and the closing of the book of sigils.

Notes

1. Maurice Merleau-Ponty, *Signs*, trans. Richard C. McCleary (Chicago: Northwestern University Press, 1964), 39.

2. For a provocative meditation along these lines, see Marian Hobson, "History Traces," in Derek Attridge, Geoff Bennington, and Robert Young, *Post-structuralism and the Question of History* (Cambridge: Cambridge University Press, 1987), 101-15. For a general overview of the background of Lacan and the post-structuralist movement, see Edith Kurzweil, *The Age of Structuralism: Levi-Strauss to Foucault* (New York: Columbia University Press, 1980).

3. See Michel Foucault, *The Order of Things: An Archaeology of the Human Sciences* (New York: Pantheon Books, 1971).

4. Jacques Lacan, *The Four Fundamental Concepts of Psycho-analysis*, trans. Alan Sheridan (New York: W.W. Norton, 1981), 188.

5. Lacan *Four Fundamental Concepts*, 188.

6. Lacan, *Ecrits: A Selection*, trans. Alan Sheridan (New York: W.W. Norton, 1977), 269.

7. For a structuralist exposition of the Heraclitean fragments, see Raymond Adolph Prier, *Archaic Logic: Symbol and Structure in Parmenides, and Empedocles* (The Hague: Mouton, 1976) 57f.

8. Lacan, *Four Fundamental Concepts*, 25.

9. Aleister Crowley, *Magick in Theory and Practice* (New York: Dover Publications, 1976), 71.

10. Ibid., 71.

11. Plato, *Phaedrus*, 275a.

12. Ibid., 275d-275e.

13. For a discussion of the ancient theory of correspondences and its effect on Western thought, see Liselotte Dieckmann, *Hieroglyphics: The History of a Literary Symbol* (St. Louis, Mo: Washington University Press, 1970), and Francis Yates, *The Art of Memory* (Chicago: University of Chicago Press, 1966).

14. Lacan, *Four Fundamental Concepts*, 258. It should be noted that Freud also understood the "dream work" undertaken by the unconscious as due to a "demonic element." See Sigmund Freud, *On Dreams*, trans. James Strachey (New York: W.W. Norton, 1952), 95.

15. Lacan, *Ecrits*, 263.

16. Sigmund Freud, *Studies in Parapsychology* (New York: Collier Books, 1963), 50.

17. Claude Levi-Strauss, *Structural Anthropology* (Garden City, N.Y.: Doubleday, 1967), 199.

18. Frederic Jameson, *The Political Unconscious: Narrative as a Socially Symbolic Act* (Ithaca, N.Y.: Cornell University Press, 1981), 19.

19. Ibid., 102.

20. Ibid., 285.

21. Lacan, *Four Fundamental Concepts*, 154. A similar interpretation is offered by Rene Girard, who sees desire as the hidden metaphysics behind all action and representation in modern literature. See *Deceit, Desire, and the Novel*, trans. Yvonne Freccero (Baltimore: Johns Hopkins University Press, 1965).

Works Cited

Attridge, Derek, Geoff Bennington, and Robert Young. *Post-Structuralism and the Question of History*. Cambridge: Cambridge University Press, 1987.

Crowley, Aleister. *Magick in Theory and Practice*. New York: Dover Publications, 1976.

Dieckmann, Liselotte. *Hieroglyphics: The History of a Literary Symbol*. St. Louis, Mo.: Washington University Press, 1970.

Foucault, Michel. *The Order of Things: An Archaeology of the Human Sciences*. New York: Pantheon Books, 1971.

Freud, Sigmund. *On Dreams*. Trans. James Strachey. New York: W.W. Norton, 1952.

_____. *Studies in Parapsychology*. New York: Collier Books, 1963.

Freccero, Yvonne. *Deceit, Desire, and the Novel*. Trans. Yvonne Freccero. Baltimore: Johns Hopkins University Press, 1965.

Hobson, Marian. "History Traces." In Derek Atridge, Geoff Bennington, and Robert Young. *Post-Structuralism and the Question of History*. Cambridge: Cambridge University Press, 1987.

Jameson, Frederic. *The Political Unconsciousness: Narrative as a Socially Symbolic Act*. Ithaca, New York: Cornell University Press, 1981.

Kurzweil, Edith. *The Age of Structuralism: Levi-Strauss to Foucault*. New York: Columbia University Press, 1980.

Lacan, Jacques. *Ecrits: A Selection*. Trans. Alan Sheridan. New York: W.W. Norton, 1981.

_____. *The Four Fundamental Concepts of Psychoanalysis*. Trans. Alan Sheridan. New York: W.W. Norton, 1981.

Levi-Strauss, Claude. *Structural Anthropology*. Garden City, N.Y.: Doubleday, 1967.

Merleau-Ponty, Maurice. *Signs*. Trans. Richard C. McCleary. Chicago: Northwestern University Press, 1964.

Plato, *Phaedrus*. Trans. R. Hackforth in *The Collected Dialogue of Plato*. Ed. Edith Hamilton and Huntington Cairns (Princeton, N.J.: Princeton University Press, 1961).

Prier, Adolph. *Archaic Logic: Symbol and Structure in Parmenides and Empedocles*. The Hague: Mouton, 1976.

Yates, Francis. *The Art of Memory*. Chicago: University of Chicago Press, 1966.

Summary

David Crownfield

Carl Raschke, as well as Winquist, Taylor, and Earle, see the Lacanian deconstruction of the Cartesian subject to be pivotal to the significance of Lacan for theological language. In Raschke's reading, the key point is that subjectivity is not an object denoted in speech, but an introjective consequence of the mimetic structure of language itself. The Other's syntactical power "rebounds upon the formation of all 'self-conscious' representations, and thus creates the subject as God authors the world."

In a sort of return from this formation of the subject through language, it is the dark intentionality of desire, in its interplay with the logic of the text, that generates the dynamics of signification. The split in the subject stands forth in the polarity of primal repression and re-presentation. This split is the origin of the unconscious, and the palingenesis of desire. In recognition of the ambiguity/ambivalence thus situated at the heart of signification, there opens a path leading toward disenchantment, toward demystification of the magical element in language.

Raschke's notion of magic requires particular attention. "Whatever is 'magic' presupposes a secrecy that by definition cannot be either contemplated or made a predicate." There is a secret mode of signification, a supplement, which is an impediment to ordinary straightforward intelligibility. It is the power of the secret referent, the secret signified, the occult subject, that is the power of magic. It rests on the forgetfulness of the introjective origin of the subject, and pursues the agendas of the imaginary in the syntax and lexicon of the symbolic.

This discussion of magical discourse belongs in relation to Julia Kristeva's post-Lacanian conception of *semiotic* discourse. She speaks of "mobile psychic inscriptions, subject to the primary processes of 'displacement' and 'condensation.'" (*Au commencement était l'amour:*

psychanalyse et foi[14]). Kristeva has in mind here the signifying force of all sorts of symbolizations, symptoms, and parapraxes, psychosomatic and behavioral, not merely linguistic. But she explicitly includes the use of the system of syntax and signification in the service of desire, where its metonymies and metaphors are governed by the imperatives of the occultation and evocation of desire, rather than primarily by the semantic functions of symbolic discourse. Magical discourse as Raschke describes it is a systematic manipulation of the symbolic in the service of the imaginary: symbolic and indeed representational in style but imaginary in function. Systematic mystification is a requisite for the effectiveness of this manipulation. (The key issue for theological discourse, in this respect is, of course, whether theology should be understood as a mode of magic or as something else. Raschke doesn't say.)

One of Raschke's most important contributions is his illumination of this concept of magical discourse through a contrast with deconstruction. Both center on, and derive their energy from, the unsaid. But in deconstruction the effect comes from the unmasking of the unsaid, its being made to "stand and deliver" through the exploitation of silences, ruptures, stress lines in the text. Magic, to the contrary, depends on masking, reifying but constantly displacing the object of desire, concealing its operations and effects under a pretext that the subject and object of desire are substantial and available, but never here and now. One of the effects of the magical manipulation is the sense of the *uncanny* it disposes of. Following Freud, Raschke roots the uncanny in the effacement of the distinction between imagination and reality, and thus in the split origin of the self.

This analysis of magic enables Raschke to make some useful criticisms of other modes of thinking. Noting the structuralist assumption that the recurrent regularities of narrative, ritual, and behavior derive from an "eternal, *transformational* agency of the unconscious," Raschke argues that structuralism has grasped only one aspect of the process. Its attention to enduring (perhaps not "timeless") patterns and their laws of transformation grasps the transpersonal dimensions of mythico-symbolic activity, but fails to see the significance of the semantic conversions involved in the passage from the unconscious to social cognition. He proposes that we must understand the structural regularities not as unconscious registers of meaning, but as transpositional keys (something like a transformational syntax of substitutions and displacements within which the metonymies and metaphors of desire can be given a viable semiotic role within the semantic manipulation of the language). Jung's archetypal structures, which Raschke does not mention, clearly can and probably should be read in this way; I do not know enough Lévi-Strauss to judge how well this concept of transpositional keys can function with respect to his anthropological structuralism.

Raschke's approach also generates a criticism of Frederick Jameson's project of integrating post-modern analysis of texts with a Marxist emphasis on the primacy of the historical character of reality, through the concept of social mediation. As Raschke reads Jameson, it is history that refuses desire and sets limits to praxis, as a sort of necessity reified, totalized, mystified. The revolution is a promise that desire can be fulfilled. But in Lacan, desire is unreifiable, unattainable, the generator and the subverter of intelligibility itself. In this light the Marxist approach to demystification of discourse is itself essentially magical.

The Lacanian analysis of the artifactuality and incoherence of the self, and the situation of desire as the irreducible expression of that incoherence, is for Raschke the end of ideology, the demystification of the magical. But what of the theological? Is this analysis itself exemplary of a theological discourse after Lacan?

Raschke reads Lacan somewhat differently from either Winquist or Taylor, with more attention to the unrealism of desire and to the way in which the imaginary is played out semiotically in the world of discourse. Does he, nevertheless, end in a view of theology as unrestrained demystification? As with Winquist, I would like to see Raschke reflect on the relation between the discourse he presents and the texts that have already been called theological discourse, and give some account of how the term 'theological' makes the passage from its role in those contexts to what it might be after Lacan.

4.

The Pathology of the Father's Rule: Lacan and the Symbolic Order

Charles E. Scott

"Discontinuity . . . is the essential form in which the unconscious first appears to us as a phenomenon—discontinuity in which something is manifested as a vacillation. . . .[I] Is there a One anterior to discontinuity? I do not think so, and everything I have been taught in recent years has tended to exclude the need for a closed One . . . a sort of double of the organism in which this false unity is thought to reside. You will grant me that the One that is introduced by the experience of the unconscious is the One of cleavage . . . of rupture. . . . Rupture, cleavage . . . make absence emerge—just as the cry does not stand out against a background of silence, but on the contrary makes silence emerge as silence."

—J. Lacan

"No cure can be effective if it remains captive to images and to the psychological images which preside over the patient's alienation."
—Antoine Vergote

The question of identity and difference has had an unusually formative power in the last twenty-five years in the West. Its previous history involves the appearance of the infinite in the finite, God in contingent circumstances, essence in instances, nature in the creature, the absolute in phases, law in rules, etc. But more recently the issue has taken a turn toward the structure and function of language. The conviction which defines the issue may be broadly stated: speaking is hidden by the spoken. To articulate a question, for example, to give it definite, enclosed status as question, forecloses the freedom of language which is enacted *as* question.[1] Language as enactment is always different from any identity that is attributed to it, a thought found in various forms in both Heidegger and Lacan. The problem is also conceived by Lacan in terms of the absence of the present Other or as the primary repression of Language by the emergence of ego-identity with its limiting and fixating needs relative to its own survival.

What has pushed some thinkers beyond the conceptuality and terminology of, for example, *Being and Time*, or beyond structuralistic methodologies, has been the issue of how to maintain alertness to this difference, as well as openness for the "voice" of this difference in how we speak. When one's thinking is formed in the speaking/spoken difference or in the signifier/signified difference, truth for thinking and as thinking cannot take the form of assertion or relations among claims, much less of correspondence between propositions and objects. Truth happens on the boundary of speaking and the spoken or of signifier and signified, and that boundary usually involves decentering the spoken's or the signifier's identity in relation to reality or being. An indefinite transcendence occurs through the difference that destructures any presumed authority of the constituted identity to function as a model, image, or analogical base for thinking about what things share in common. This difference of signifier and signified occasions a fading, a kind of dying, on the part of the identity.

That pattern has its most recent and obvious heritage in the various Hegelian traditions. But in Heidegger's or Lacan's formulations there is nothing that properly can be designated Absolute or Spirit that gives meaning to the diremptive process by advancing syntheses or by a determinant eschatology. Where the "voice" of the Absolute was once discerned, the "voice" of Language is now heard, and it is a "voice" to which no one can give full voice. It cannot be articulated satisfactorily because as speaking it cannot be spoken in determinate articulations without losing its own difference from any and all determinations. Language is articulate in hiddenness as well as in disclosure. The question arises whether the very idea of identity can be used appropriately with regard to language in its difference from any and all articulations. Lacan, for example, has not intended to give "the Unconscious" an identity. It "speaks" in difference, violation, vacillation, discontinuity. But the discourse he uses, particularly in his sexual imagery, and in his way of seeing "the Unconscious" as "like a language," betrays the nonidentity of "the Unconscious."

We shall question Lacan's notion of the Symbolic Order, termed the Law of the Father, in light of the issue of identity and difference. Symbolic Order functions in his thinking like an ineffable identity in relation to the masculine symbols and images that he utilizes. Within the context of an original understanding of identity and difference, he

perpetuates a remarkably traditional image of dominant male authority for interpreting both language and human development. This consequence is opposed to his best intentions, as expressed, for example,
in the epigraph above. This dominant male imagery referring to the
Symbolic Order means that the authority of language is like a masculine authority. This way of speaking considerably compromises one of
his most distinctive and significant contributions: a way of speaking of
unconscious dimensions outside of the influences and affections of
Western theism. His male imagery also has the effect of subjecting
feminine imagery to its authority, and consequently of limiting those
ways of thinking in which the nonmasculine and nonauthoritative
aspects of language and life have organizing influence in our discourses
and desires.

Schreber and the Father's Rule

We begin with a case history provided by Freud that Lacan has
made central in his own modifications of Freud. Our specific goal is to
hear through Lacan's interpretation of this case how he conceives the
issue of the ontological difference between Language and speech. With
which symbols does he find the Symbolic? Which words bear the violations by which the Unconscious, the Other, becomes manifest? Our
larger intention is twofold: to discover the symbolism in the Lacanian
discourse, and to find how he conceives this symbolism, how these
symbols work themselves through his discourse as a site of paternal
symbolization. We shall begin with Richardson's summary of the
Schreber Case:

> Daniel Paul Schreber (1824-1911) was the son of an illustrious father
> whose conception of pedagogy earned him a permanent place in the
> history of nineteenth-century educational theory. Trained as a lawyer
> and functioning as a local judge, he had his first bout with madness
> at the age of forty-two after failing in his candidacy for member-
> ship in the Reichstag. He suffered from "severe hypochondria" and
> was admitted to a clinic in Leipzig, where for eight months he was
> under the care of Dr. Paul Emil Flechsig. After discharge he man-
> aged to remain functional for eight years. At the age of fifty-one there
> was trouble again, just six months after he had been elected Presid-
> ing Judge of the Court of Appeals in Dresden. Despite the profes-
> sional success, he was severely disappointed when it became clear
> that his wife was incapable of bearing a child. At any rate, in October,
> 1893 he suffered a severe anxiety attack, attempted suicide and soon
> was readmitted to Flechsig's Clinic. After eight months he was trans-

ferred to the clinic at Sonnenstein, where he remained legally committed for almost nine years. Finally he contested the legal commitment and helped draft the case that argued successfully for his discharge, or at least for change of status to a "voluntary" commitment. The *Memoirs* were written during that nine-year commitment and trace the course of his illness.

The *Memoirs* were not planned as a book but were composed from jottings so as to be able to give his wife and others "at least an approximate idea of my religious conceptions so that they have some understanding of the necessity which forces me to various oddities of behavior."[2] The oddities included the habit of wearing cheap jewelry, ribbons, or other feminine ornaments for several hours a day, and attacks of compulsive bellowing if the ritual that these accoutrements were supposed to accompany was impeded.[3]

A more detailed account of the phenomenon comes from the report of the attending physician:

The patient's delusional system amounts to this: he is called to redeem the world and to bring back to mankind the lost state of Blessedness. He maintains he has been given this task by direct divine inspiration, similar to that taught by the prophets; he maintains that nerves in a state of excitation, as his have been for a long time, have the property of attracting God, but it is a question of things which are either not at all expressible in human language or only with great difficulty, because he maintains they lie outside all human experience and have only been revealed to him. The most essential part of his mission of redemption is that it is necessary for him first of all to be transformed into a woman. Not, however, that he wishes to be transformed into a woman, it is much more a "must" according to the Order of the World, which he simply cannot escape, even though he would personally very much prefer to remain in his honorable manly position in life. But the beyond was not to be gained again for himself and the whole of mankind other than by this future transformation into a woman by way of divine miracle in the course of years or decades. He maintains that he is the exclusive object of divine miracles, and with it the most remarkable human being that ever lived on earth. For years at every hour and every minute he experienced these miracles in his body, has them confirmed also by voices that speak to him. He maintains that in the earlier years of his illness he suffered destruction of individual organs of his body, of a kind which would have brought death to every other human being, that he lived for a long time without stomach, without intestines, bladder, almost without lungs, with

smashed ribs, torn gullet, that he had at times eaten part of his own
larynx with his food, etc.; but divine miracles ("rays") had always
restored the destroyed organs, and therefore, as long as he remained
a man, he was absolutely immortal. These threatening phenomena
have long ago disappeared, and in their place his "femaleness" had
come to the fore; it is a question of an evolutionary process which in
all probability will take decades if not centuries for its completion
and the end of which is unlikely to be witnessed by any human being
now alive. He has the feeling that already masses of "female nerves"
have been transferred into his body, from which through immediate
fertilization by God new human beings would come forth. Only then
would he be able to die a natural death and have gained for himself
as for all other human beings the state of Blessedness. In the mean-
time not only the sun but also the trees and the birds, which he thinks
are something like "remains of previous human souls transformed by
miracles", speak to him in human tones and everywhere around him
miracles are enacted.[4]

Our interest is in Lacan's interpretation of the structure of Language (the Other, the Unconscious), in this case of psychosis. Although
Lacan's is a remarkably nonlinear use of language—his is a discourse of
allusions, symbolizations, and intuitive leaps—his interest is also in
explanation. He wants to explain the origin of psychosis, and in this
case of a psychosis in which a man feels divinely called to be a woman.
Lacan also is a part of the Western metaphysical tradition's desire to be
a rigorous science, a desire that moved Plato as much as Kant and
Husserl. The relations among the differences of hallucinations, non-
hallucinatory experiences, male and female, order and absence of order
(Lacan calls the absence of order in this context the "mother-infant
dyad")—these relations are to be understood and, with regard to psychosis, explained. We shall not ask if Lacan's explanation is accurate.
We shall note the discourse, the use of words, by which he explains
and interprets.

The movement is as follows: the infant and mother are in an
undifferentiated bond, an All Lacan calls it at times, that is not linguistic or symbolic, not conscious or unconscious. When the child begins
to speak, this bond is broken by the intrusion of Language, the symbolic structure of relations that makes individual articulation possible.
Language bears through speech a vast network of inevitabilities that,
as a completely impersonal and unloving destiny, interrupts, savagely
one assumes, the mother-infant All. Whereas the mother-infant dyad
is a sealed closeness, Language is the inevitability of distance, of the
presence and absence of the signifier in the signified, in which the All

can be no more than a memory of desire. It is a powerful memory, a symbolic ideal repressed in and by the advent of language, and one the child being initiated into speech yearns to recover. How is the distance from the signified, in this case the mother, to be overcome? The distance is too great, like a line of chaos, and cannot be bridged by the now speaking child. But if the child is desired by the mother, if the child can be sought by the mother as her fulfillment, the reunion might be effected. She lacks and desires a phallus. The Phallus, the signifier of desire, the desiring, and the desired, however, is a Symbol—not merely an individually concocted image but a signifier originating in the involuntary event of becoming a creature of Language, a signifier that already articulates a distance from the signified. This articulation of distance restates the initiating situation in which distance first originated. It means both distance and drive to overcome distance. An iron Law is at work, the inevitability of presence *and* absence in language, a destiny repeated in the symbolic struggle to overcome it, and this signifier of desire, the Phallus, thus fails in its ur-mission. Its failure is part of the symbolic occurrence. Its failure means not only that the primal desire for union without distance or absence or dialectic cannot be; it also means that the Law, the procreator of human beings, viz. of speaking creatures, this Law-as-procreator is the symbolic Father, also symbolized phallically, who overwhelms the child's union with the mother and whose presence is meant by the absent mother and the consequent desire. The Law-as-Father has cut off mother-child union, and the symbolic power of the Phallus, as the Symbol of desire, originates in this intrusion. Hence the Phallus has a pivotal role in the symbolic process by which the subject and the Other (Language) come to be. The Phallus means the lost and hence desired mother, and it means as well the Law-as-Father, the necessity of separation, the Other which is the nether One, which has no other, no clear reflection, no shadow, and which occurs nonetheless as the Father's Name for the linguistic creature. It is a hard beginning for us all.

In Schreber's case, something in the symbolic process went awry. For some reason the castration did not develop, and Schreber, that particular individual, did not have the possibility of allowing the Name of the Father to emerge and to be Other. (Both Freud and Lacan ignore Schreber's relation to his biological father. Neither appears to notice, also, that the analysis is based solely on heavily censored documents.) This strange symbolic lapse characterized the Other-with-Schreber, and as the possibility for his imaginal life the Name of the Father was imprinted, not as a violating Other but as a hole, a deficiency in how he could imagine and experience the world. The hole in the symbolic network was lived out by Schreber as the divine command to be a woman, and as the apparent absence of Law in his imaginary world; his own mother's apartment was the place of his beginning insanity. In the absence of castration Schreber's world lacked also the desire-signifier (Phallus) that linked him to the Law of Language and to the *distant* mother; hence he became a desire for the Phallus, a desire to be woman, and the imagery of that desire, in the absence of effective, symbolic castration, was wild, hallucinatory, crazy. He could not individually establish a productive, fathering relation with the Other—no one can. The Other "is not at the disposal of the subject in reestablishing the continuity of the conscious discourse."[4] And, in the absence of castration, he had no Father to be his Other. Without the Father, in the absence of effective Symbolic destiny, his discourse was merely imaginary.

In Lacan's remarkable theory there is a thorough ambivalence regarding the Other. On the one hand it is alterity as such. It is not any one thing, certainly, but is a chain of signifiers within a chain of signifiers, and so on. But this chaining, if we may call it that, is ruled/ruling. It is Law, a network of signifiers that spells an inevitability so vast, so originally procreative that it is not susceptible to any set of signifiers. But this alterity is also not to be appropriated by meditation or wisdom or a culmination of self-actualization. It is recognizable as Law and rule-governed Destiny, which seems to mean that it is nameable as Name of the Father or as Symbolic Order. We many never get the Father under our belts, as it were. We may never become it or grasp it within the limits of our words and images—it is always back of our speaking, in our speaking, beyond our speaking. But it is Other. Not the Derridean, ⊀ t⊀e Ot⊀er, I believe, but Other. Not *différance*, but the continual differencing that is strangely accessible to the disciplined thought and investigation of some linguists and psychoanalysts. The ambiguity is that the Other is totally different formally from the theological claim that God is He who is totally beyond us and is yet the subject of theology that we can be right about, even unto His essence.

Identity and The Same

Lacan's writing has the effect of keeping the reader off balance and uncertain about what is being said. That difficulty is one way by which Lacan intends to occasion the Other's being apparent as Signifier that is slashed (S/s) (always) in relation to the signified. The difficulty of his writing is itself like the slash. It makes grasping a "core" or an essence impossible, so the theories that Lacan propounds, when their articulation is heard and appropriated, cannot be taken as sufficient for their subject. If, for example, the present discussion of Lacan were found to be clear, and the reader felt that by understanding it he or she had an adequate hold on an aspect of Lacan's thought, that aspect, so understood, would be a signified that is unslashed in relation to the signifier (s means S). Whatever the difference between the understood and the occurrence of Lacan's thinking and speaking, that difference would be taken to be insignificant as far as our sense of clarity is concerned. We would experience ourselves as having a hold on Lacan, an understanding relation with his discourse; but the Other, as he conceived it, would seem to be left out of our understanding, and our understanding would consequently be superficial.

By this style Lacan intends to make more likely the appearance of the Other through our reading him. The psychoanalyst at best keeps the Unconscious in mind, staying open for the Unconscious's way of appearing through the discourse of the patient. And in Lacan's practice the Other is heard through breaks, slips, and the way the discourse is troubled and unsettled. If one is at ease in his or her language, confident or thoroughly caught up in what he or she is saying, the analyst's task is to provide an interruption, by his efforts to hear the Other rather than the patient's self-assurance. The difficulty of Lacan is that interruption in our intellectual cultivation of understanding.

The Name of the Father, then, whose presence is symbolized, in part, by the Phallus, emerges in a dual movement in Lacan's writing: it is signified by Lacan's theories, and it appears through the violation that his style effects in our discourse and in the tradition of his own discourse. The Father's rule is not found in an airtight system, a logic of process, or any other form of ratiocination that is presumed to constitute adequacy of knowledge. That rule is found through a process like castration, when the agency of our desire to establish a full and satisfying relationship with something known is eliminated by a rupture through which a Rule is revealed, a Rule as far beyond our grasp and agency as the father's penis is beyond the agency of the little boy.

Given the primary importance of Lacan's style for his interpretation of the Other, we should not confuse what he speaks of as Other with the occurrence of Other. The Rule of the Father does not happen as a signified, nor does Its occurrence with us find Its completion in noesis-like contemplation. The expectation of some type of reunion, of any kind of relation articulated by symbols of nurturance, growth with attachment, dwelling in peace, feminine fertility, interplay free of conflict, serene intimacy, or being together free of the history of violence — any such symbols are not only foreign to Lacan in his discourse; they mean, if they tell us about the Symbolic System, a serious misalignment with the Father's Rule.

The symbolic Father, then, is like an ineffable identity in Lacan's discourse. He is not like a desiring person or an awesome character. He

is like an ungraspable symbolic process in action in some limited articulation of that process. The Rule of Symbols in Language, not the
person, is the proper reference when we think about Law, and that
Rule is like an Identity that makes differences, when lesser identities
simultaneously express It and fall short of It. Only by accepting this
Rule will we be able to speak and think appropriately as nonruling
parts of this paternal whole.

The signifying-whole/signified-part relation is expressed for Lacan
in disclosure and hiddenness which, when taken together, mean an
unalterable foreignness dwelling in all that is familiar to us. In Lacan's
myth of human genesis, the infant is wrenched from its undifferentiated
presence with its need-fulfilling mother. Totality, or at least its sense of
totality, is sundered. This sundering occurs as Language enters the infant's experience, and with It comes desire for the (illusion of) pure being,
i.e., being-with-mother-fulfillment, the unending search for an other by
whom one is totally desired and whom one can satisfy totally. The *impossibility* in this search for an other is *disclosive* of the Other, who, in His
Vastness and Inscrutable Destiny, is *hidden*. When the Other is heard
in this impossible dream, one can see that his or her desire is of the
Other, the not-an-other. The hidden presence of the Symbolic Father, a
hiddenness that is revealed in the presence of rupture and lack, means
that desire will not be satisfied by anything, that our desire is infinite
for all practical purposes. The Law of the Father is articulated always
in a chain of signifiers that has no completion. Further, desire as the
desire-to-be originates in rupture—castration symbolizes the birth of desire—and one consequently finds that his or her desire for Other is like,
perhaps, the Other-as-desire for which there is no fulfillment because
it is a process of desire, a Rule of desire without hope of completion.

When we say that Other is like a nonpersonal, desiring identity,
we must keep in mind that Other is darkly articulated in a "dialectic of
desire" that has no culmination, no eschaton in its future. But Other
does appear in aspects of Lacan's speech to be like identity, in spite of
Its lack of determinateness, because Lacan finds the best symbols in
the Rule of the Father and in the Phallus.

By contrast, Foucault, for example, locates rule and destiny within
history and accounts for them through histories of practices, institutions, and discourses. The Same is not found in the recurrence of order,
but in the fragmented origins of orders which constitute destinies for
specific groups of people. Orders are not Ordered. Looking for an
overarching order, recognizing Father in the transcendence of Language,
or finding infinity in desire—all those acts (looking, recognizing, finding) are themselves expressions of orders, of discourses that have origins, durations, and declines. The Same for Foucault, were he to use

the term, would be like absence without Rule, or emptiness without specificity. The central symbolization of the Father's Rule and the Phallus would not arise, because the contingency pervasive in his way of thinking does not generate the symbolic dominance of the cultural male or of Other-beyond-signification. Generation is more closely allied with accident, specific structures of power and practice, given authorities, and particular rules, than with Necessity and Authority. Rupture is the appearance of nothing necessary in the midst of all of the necessities of our lives. Absence is not like a symbolic Father's castrating his symbolic son in the desire of a symbolic mother; absence is like an image of a mad person pervaded by shadows and spears of light, or Athena emerging from the head of Zeus suspended in air. For our purposes we need to underscore the possibility of conceiving absence without the symbolic overtones of vast identity-like Order, and to note that in this possibility, male-dominated symbolization of alterity ceases.

When the Same is conceived without Order or Rule, merger or symbiosis is not an attractive symbolic alternative. Human beings may certainly experience difficulties that have to do with interruption of various mother-child relationships. We may also suffer from illusions of being able to be embodied without identity or responsibility, in a total merger with something absolutely satisfying. The issue we are addressing, however, has to do with determinate symbolization, focused on symbolic identities and on analogies with identity. Lacan makes family relationships the region for symbolization, and his discourse is defined by symbolic paternal family structures in which the inexpressibleness and unencompassableness of the rule that defines relatedness dominates: that kind of experience in which one finds oneself forever expressing the very rule that one is trying to destroy or ignore or differentiate. Levinas, by contrast, also gives emphasis to the family, but he makes dwelling and home the central phenomena for understanding same and other. He finds that recognition (not the desire to be desired), intimacy (neither a symbiotic nor a castrating experience), gentleness (not violation), familiarity (coming together out of separateness), and welcome (coming to oneself in hospitality) are the deepest or highest dimensions of the human family. In his discourse the other happens as countenance, as face and as facing, as an utterly concrete (as well as preverbal) personal encounter. According to Levinas, relatedness does not arise out of Rule or out of symbiosis: relatedness is a nonreducible given. Whoever is most and least accurate, however, and whoever leads us to a manner of speaking and being by which 'I' and 'other' come most to themselves in expression, both Levinas and Lacan give emphasis to identities within the sameness of family life by their use of sexual and domestic symbols and images. But the family unit of sameness-with-difference, and sameness that is either paternally or maternally imaged, is not adequate for interrupting difference and indeterminancy.

Our dominant traditions are shadowed by a memory of discourses with multiple powers or gods, none of whom manages to rule all the others. To speak of Ariadne in 900 B.C., for example, was also to mean Dionysus, probably, but not necessarily Zeus. She probably meant labyrinth and death, but not necessarily Hades or Persephone. With her discourse one felt no reason to urge symbolic unity or a dominance of identity. Such memories are a part, if a sedimented part, of our tradition's discourse, parts to which we cannot return as though we were not where and who we are, but discourses which remind us of the shadows and probably the fears in our traditional search for the rules by which I and other must abide in order to be. Ariadne reminds us that the image of labyrinth may have more to do with rule as such, than with the signification of Rule, as Lacan's discourse has it.

The shadows and fears of our tradition have the power to dislodge the negative and positive passions that empower the dominant and definitive interests of any given time. The idea of Same without Rule or Identity, with its freedom from the symbolization of paternal rule, gives voice to a memory of discourse without a desire for unity, a discourse in which orders were multiple and continuously decentered by other rule-orientations that featured entirely different inevitabilities. Each grouping developed its own manner of symbolizing, and lest one discover Unity in symbolization itself, together they left their differences intercepted by nothing to be spoken or symbolized: Same without Identity, symbolic or literal.

Lacan approximates this type of insight by his emphasis on otherness as such, as distinct from an other. His discourse is remarkably freeing in relation to those fixations of language that occur when a way of thinking and speaking is abstracted from desire, and when one speaks literally as though free of decentering alterity. He listens as he writes and speaks for the occurrence of difference, for the radical qualification of each instance of identity or meaning. But the Rule of the Father haunts his freedom, as Lacan expected it to; it creates an ineffable, symbolic identity of desire that makes the slash between signifying and signified a revelation of Other instead of absence of I and Other. In that way our preoccupation with both Identity and its paternity receive a refined expression.

Pathology

I have entitled this discussion "The Pathology of the Father's Rule." Lacan's analysis of Schreber's psychosis claims that his illness is due to an absence of symbolic castration, as we have seen. The fissure created by castration, the slash, is to be kept if one is to avoid psychosis. The *paternitas interrupta* introduces the ironic completeness of human being under the Father's Rule. This myth functions in a way similar to the Christian/Hebraic myth of the Fall in the sense that it tells us about our human origin, claims that the origin happens with a loss of a sense of unmediated union, and through the origin finds the Father to be present and absent as ineffable Law, Law that makes possible and defines all relationships and human expression. Only when this scission is fully a part of one's life, not denied, for example, by an egocentric web of fixed and rigid relations in a vain effort to construct a life without dialectic and rupture—rather, only in the lived consciousness of scission will a human life be fully its own: lived in attention to Other, in freedom for and in finite violations, the unsolvable interplay of desire, and the incompleteness of its being.

Lacan's myth, so thoroughly a part of the Freudian discourse, has a controlling image of, as it were, Deity. It has a powerful understanding of freedom, but a freedom-with-Other, a freedom-in-the-Name-of-the-Father. His brilliant innovation of using language and symbolization to replace biology and to modify the notion of urge, even urge that is controlled by the singular image of the Father's ineffable Rule. But suppose there *is* such a Rule. Suppose that Language *does* happen like the Name-of-the-Father. Suppose the phallus *is* the dominant symbol of desire, at least in our tradition. Myth and symbol aside, suppose that Lacan is *right*.

Such suppositions are misplaced even in a positive relation to Lacan. He is not claiming empirical accuracy. He is showing that empirical accuracy cannot be true, given truth's labyrinthine (his image) and breaching way of occurring. The issue is one of symbolic relations, of Language's happening, of the interplay of I and Other. We are not in a lab or even a scholar's world. We are in the processes by which people lose and find themselves through language—not an empirical process, but rather a real one, full of symbols, contradictions, transcendence, and truths, without the problem of accuracy or inaccuracy. Because the occurrences of language (not its "nature") are in question, our task is to speak of, to, and with Language. Our task is to enter discourse with maximum awareness in order to address the subject of Lacan's discourse. This task is particularly difficult if one speaks a discourse considerably different from Lacan's. Although we are not attempting to speak within the symbolic and imaginal limits of the Freudian discourse, we are nonetheless able to consider the issue of pathology in terms of language.

Our observation is twofold: the Father's Rule involves an inadequate cluster of images with which to speak of our relation with language, and when this cluster dominates, our relation to language is severely constricted.

The history of the Father's Rule would doubtlessly show a lineage of limiting choices, exclusions, fear, and constrained experience, as well as insight and alertness. We shall limit ourselves to observing, however, the singularity of the Father's rule in understanding Language, a singularity that appears to offer domination of difference rather than its free allowance. Heidegger's phrase, the granting of difference in the Same, points out a missing dimension in Lacan's work: differences are subsumed under or incorporated by the symbolic Rule of the Father. The direction of the symbolic Phallus is phallic: in creating difference, in granting difference, in separating I and Other, it means an object-creating desire. One desires and consequently one desires to be desired. That is essentially the meaning of the desire to be (or the want of being). But the Phallus is not the space that it enters. Desire, according to Lacan, is searching, positing, forever repeating its own origins in incision. Most of what comes to us culturally as feminine, or at least as not male, is for Lacan like the element through which the Phallus extends: space for movement, nurturance, the intimacy of dwelling, nonlinear, labyrinthine desire and consciousness, giving birth, womb-like fecundity — in short, being feminine (regardless of physical sex) is being vaguely but persistently ruled by the Father, who though he might be conceived with a greater emphasis on aspects not culturally male, is not regularly conceived that way by Lacan. His style could transgress the masculine bias, but even in his nonlinear style, which recognizes the darkness and mystery of truth, for example, Lacan operates by assertion, incisiveness, criticism, formalization, contestation, etc.

This bias for fatherly singularity brings us to the final observation: in Lacan's discourse, the differences from Father appear to be so phallically overridden and so important in their unruled differences in our history, that we expect this discourse, in spite of its power of insight, to make likely its own kind of pathology, a pathology of the Father's Rule. Lacan's discourse is not hostile to the world; it is committed to our being with the Real without world-distorting illusions and images. But there is in it nonetheless a hostility to *dwelling*. Levinas and Heidegger use this word, albeit in subtly different ways. I do not use the word to suggest that Lacan should agree with one or the other of them, but to name a dimension of our heritage that is pathologically overridden in the Lacanian discourse. "Dwelling" connotes safety and nurturance, that kind of freedom that maximizes identity with difference, and preservation through affirmation, kindness, and affection. To dwell, to grow, and to be one's own being are associated in our language. Learning to be who one is in relation to another and in relation to one's being, in a situation of maximum allowance and trust, is an essential part of many therapies, and could be taken as learning how to dwell and allow dwelling. In the imagery of dwelling, in contrast to the imagery of the Father's Rule, the interplay is not originated by symbolic castration but by granting and gathering differences, by nurturance without fusion or symbiosis, with a sameness that gives place for difference and relation. This discourse of dwelling is open to the emergence of all manner of powers: impossible desires, stolid defensiveness, waterlike play of feelings, tragic conflicts, etc. It has the disadvantage of lacking clear and straightforward prescriptiveness and the power to resolve significant conflicts by direct action or intervention. It cannot tell people what to do or who to be. It is not a discourse of techniques that informs us helpfully how to evaluate and achieve goals. It is inadequate for analyzing power-relations. It has many other important limits. But it also has the advantage in the present context of providing no tendency to establish itself as the dominant symbolizing power for language and being. If it controls, it does so by relativizing anything in its region through its affirmation of the thing's (or the other discourse's) way of being, its boundaries, its being simply as it is. The logos of maximizing and nurturing differences, rather than the logos of insistence and assertion, allows the differences to individuate, to speak for themselves, to hear the others through the element not of the Other but of sameness without identity, which seems to be more like empty space or perhaps emptiness, than like a symbolic order. And such a discourse inclines us to think that any pretense to primary singularity represses the capacity of language to be a dwelling that grants differences and never takes sides. The Father's Rule is an insistence that exaggerates its difference into a language-forming identity, inadequately attentive to the unruled indifference of the place of its being.

The discourse of dwelling is awkward in a competitive, combative, or analytical environment. It is awkward in this paper, which is written critically. It does not encourage the kind of insistence that I have used in explaining the pathology of the Father's Rule. Its direction is toward a different way of speaking that probably would not speak in metaphors of pathology but more immediately and non-explanatorily of human need and fulfillment, their history, their speech, their differences. This discourse of dwelling does not invalidate what Lacan or I have done; but when we speak without dwelling we commit a violence in and to our language that will likely be lived in a privation of available sustenance. This sustenance is the presence of the same in dwelling, a sameness that nurtures difference but lacks both alterity and identity. The privation is experienced as the expenditure of a great deal of energy in maintaining the unnecessary violence of expressing ourselves as though we were cut off from this absence of identity that is strangely present in all our difference.

Notes

1. Jacques Derrida, *Writing and Difference*, trans. Alan Bass (Chicago: University of Chicago Press, 1978), 80.

2. William H. Richardson, "Lacan and the Problems of Psychosis" in David B. Allison, Prade de Oleivera, Mark S. Roberts and Allen S. Weiss, *Psychosis and Sexual Identity: Towards a Post-Analytic View of the Schreber Case* (Albany: State University of New York Press, 1988), 24.

3. Daniel Paul Schreber, *Memoirs of my Nervous Illness*, trans. by I. McAlpine and R.A. Hunter (London: Dawson and Sons, 1955) 1 (Republished by Harvard University Press. Pagination retained.)

4. Ibid, 386-88.

5. Jacques Lacan, *Ecrits*, Trans. Alan Sheridan (New York: W.W. Norton, 1977), 49.

Works Cited

Derrida, Jacques. *Writing and Difference*. Trans. Alan Bass. Chicago: University of Chicago Press, 1978.

Foucault, Michel. *Language, Counter-Memory, Practice*. Trans. Sherry Simon. Ithaca: Cornell University Press, 1977.

_____. *Madness and Civilization*. Trans. Sherry Simon. Ithaca, N.Y.: Cornell University Press, 1977.

Heidegger, Martin. *Being and Time*. Trans. J. Macquarrie and E. Robinson. New York: Harper and Row, 1962.

Lacan, Jacques. *Ecrits*. Trans. Alan Sheridan. New York: W.W. Norton, 1977.

Muller, J.P. and W.J. Richardson. *Lacan and Language: A Reader's Guide to the Ecrits*. New York: International Universities Press, 1982.

Summary

David Crownfield

Charles Scott poses a sharp and fruitful contrast between Lacan's thesis of the centrality of the Law or Name of the Father and an emphasis on dwelling, nurture, nonconflictual differences indebted to Heidegger and Levinas. The focus for his analysis is Lacan's discussion of the case of Daniel Paul Schreber, best known through Freud's essay on it. Schreber was a nineteenth-century jurist whose *Memoirs* recorded his delusions, including centrally his conviction that he was called to redeem the world through a process that involved his being reluctantly transformed into a woman. Lacan uses Schreber as a model for a theory of psychosis, in which the decisive problem is the failure to enter into the world of language and publicly negotiated symbols. This failure derives from the lack of an adequate experience of the symbolic phallus, the absence of the individuation that comes through being barred by the father from dyadic symbiosis with mother, and thus a failure to enter into the social world through symbolic castration. Lacking this normative sequence of developmental defeats, Schreber's symbolic world is private and insane, and he is obsessed with identification with Mother and her void rather than with phallic desire.

Scott recognizes much to appreciate in Lacan, but objects strongly to the paternal and regulative imagery of this model of human being, to which he counterposes a nonpatriarchal cluster of images that may be subsumed under that of *dwelling*. To see how this contrast is developed and what it accomplishes, let us look more closely at Scott's reading of Lacan's "origin myth" of human development.

As Scott tells Lacan's story, it begins with an undifferentiated dyadic bond of mother and child, a primordial All. When the child begins to speak, the impersonal, distancing inevitabilities of language savagely rupture this dyadic All, which subsequently exists only as memory, repressed ideal, desire. The dominant issue of life then becomes how

93

to overcome this distance, this unbridgeable failure of all signifiers to deliver the signified mother. But, if mother were to desire the child, reunion would be possible. What does mother lack and desire? The phallus! The phallus then becomes the signifier of desire, of the desired one, of the desiring one. Symbol at once of lack and of the desired reunion, it stands, irreducibly ambiguous, between restoration of the original situation and the utter remoteness from that original that is the nature of the symbolic as such. Ambiguous and merely symbolic, it fails. The law of language, of symbolic substitution, that procreator of speaking being, is symbolically Father; it is this Father that has overwhelmed the child's union with mother. Absence of mother, the essence of symbolic substitution, signifies the Father. This cutting off of union, this symbolic castration that the very phallic symbol of reunion accomplishes, is the Law of the Father. The phallus thus signifies the lost mother, the Law of the Father, the Father as the Other.

Scott's account follows Lacan closely in most respects, but at several places shifts the emphasis from where I find it in Lacan. These shifts derive largely from Scott's decision to situate the Lacanian issues in relation to questions of Identity and difference. This pair of terms, in his essay, does not focus on what makes the same the same and the different different. His concern is with questions of the One and the many, the Infinite in the finite, the essence in its instances, nature in the creature, the Absolute in its phases: an Identity that marks and rules all differences. All such totalistic integrative schemes are undesirable in Scott's view. He finds in Lacan an absolutism of the Father's Rule, a totalism of language, a concern with authority, order and rule. Acknowledging Lacan's attention to the decentering and subversive character of desire and the unconscious, Scott holds that, nevertheless, the paternal, masculine imagery reinstates the singular mastery of an Identity that dominates all difference.

As I read Lacan, the Other is represented sometimes by Mother, sometimes by Father, sometimes by the voice of the unconscious, sometimes by the sexual partner, sometimes by death. Other, in these contexts, invokes the Real unmanageable alterity that bounds our existence. Scott recognizes at several points that Other signifies alterity as such; but for the most part, he reads Lacan to identify Other with the Father's Rule taken as totalistic Identity. He argues, indeed, that the ambiguity between the totally Other and the nameable Father subverts Lacan's text; he compares it with the position of the theologian who affirms the ineffability of the divine, yet claims to have a true doctrine of God. The comparison is not trivial. Scott, by conjoining Other, Father, and Identity, makes Lacan's work a kind of theology, maintaining a theistic absolutism even though its God does not exist.

The impossibility of relating to the first other — mother — discloses the presence of the real Other, Father. The universal Rule of language implicates the subject in a vast and inscrutable Destiny, in which one's fate is rupture, castration, infinitely unfulfillable Desire. The Other is a nonpersonal desiring identity, always lost in the infinite deferrals of signification, yet always master in that its best symbols are the phallus and the Rule. Ironically, it is only in submission to the symbolic castration worked by this Other that human wholeness is possible. Freedom is only possible in the Name, under the Rule, of the Father.

What is missing here, Scott holds, is dwelling. There is a lack of images of reunion, nurturance, growth with attachment, peace, fertility, nonconflictual interplay, intimacy. The totalism of the Father's Rule is contrasted with Foucault's analysis of rules and destinies that arise, flourish, and pass away in the history of particular communities and their practices and discourses, with an emphasis on contingency, accident, particular variations. Lacan's neo-Oedipal images of family life are contrasted with Levinas's attention to home, recognition, gentleness, familiarity, welcome, hospitality. The castrating Other of symbolic Rule is contrasted with the other as countenance, face and facing, preverbal and concrete. Relatedness here is not either symbiosis or subjection to Rule; it is gift. One lives not struggling for identity but in a varying play of sameness and difference.

This context has given a different turn to the question of identity and difference. Here it is the question of self-identification, a struggle for identity, an intolerance of difference, which Scott sees still assumed (perhaps unintentionally) in Lacan. Over against this sort of identity/difference polarity, Scott affirms a variable same-and-different pair, identifying with the other freely and contingently, enjoying difference without needing to defend a threatened identity. Such a human being is not centered in identity, tied up with Law and its transgression, defined by its incompleteness and its unattainable desires. It finds space to live, in nurturance, safety, intimacy, fecundity. One is preserved through affirmation, kindness, affection, trust. We can be what we are, grow, relate, be open to emergence, allow and cherish differences.

I unreservedly join Scott in his evocation and praise of these images of dwelling. There are places in Lacan's texts that suggest that he would, too. Why, then, does Lacan present this emphasis on the Father's Rule, desire, castration, phallus, that Scott finds so inimical to dwelling? Is it merely a cultural leftover of patriarchy, or a secretly unreconstructed patriarchalism in Lacan? Or is there something else at stake? Is it necessary somehow to go by way of the Father's Rule to attain to the place, to receive the gift, of dwelling?

Reading Lacan intricates one's own self-understanding in the problems, gaps, impasses evoked in the text. Scott, indeed, claims that the difficulty of Lacan's style functions as itself an unmasterable Rule, a symbolic castration, an insuperable Other for the reader. My own reading constantly involves me in questions of desire, of castration, of Father, of who this is that reads and that wonders and whose mind wanders, of who this "unconscious" is who takes over my reading of the words and blinds and distorts and forces his agenda on my reading. It is not Lacan that makes my experience of these primordial issues a confrontation with totalistic authority, defeat and loss; it is not Lacan that makes the lure of desire continue to lead and bind me back into these struggles. How do I make the passage from this struggle and this lure to the space of dwelling? True, there is nowhere to which I have to pass; but how do I quiet the struggle so as to receive the gift? Buddhism says the way to release from suffering is through release from desire. Lacan seems to me to teach that the way to release is through acceptance of loss, through recognition of the impossibility of desire, through acceptance of the symbolic processes of displacement and substitution. It is only as barrier to desire, as marker of the still-unaccepted loss, that the Father's Rule is dominance, authority, totalization. Insofar as the impossible project can be relinquished, the obsession with this dominance can give place to dwelling.

Scott reads Lacan as carrying on a covertly theological discourse, monotheistic, patriarchal, absolutistic. In my reading, too, I find these issues, but I construe them to be a function of my own obsession with the Father's Rule and with the lure of the unfulfillable desire. I share fully Scott's evocation of the life of dwelling, but I see Lacan not as its antagonist but as one who analyzes the structure of the illusory obstacle that bars us from dwelling. It is possible that, by putting his emphasis on the obstacle, Lacan inadvertently reinforces it: that psychoanalysis, through its examination of the pathology of existence, sustains the obsession that blinds us to dwelling. Perhaps this is as far as Scott intends to drive his criticism.

But there remains a question. Is there a theological discourse in the space of dwelling? What is theology, what is the life and discourse of faith in the dwelling community? of religion? of spirituality? Neither Lacan nor Scott shows us the way to an answer, but through his confrontation of Lacan by the images of dwelling, Scott has helped us to recognize the question of its possibility.

5.

Recontextualizing the Ontological Argument: A Lacanian Analysis

Edith Wyschogrod

I read Lacan. I ask myself: what is this good for? It is good for nothing. If so, can this be proved? I will try. I will not know, you will not know, if I am successful. In Lacanian terms, if I have succeeded, I have failed; If I fail, I have succeeded. *Doch*, I shall apply Lacanian techniques to one of Western theology's most frequently and strenuously examined texts, Anselm's ontological argument. By remapping the proof, I hope, with Lacanian audacity, to bring forth unforeseen significations and a new approach to the psychoanalytic interpretation of religious texts.

One difficulty in developing a psychoanalytic discourse appropriate to theological texts arises because unconscious content has largely been viewed nondiscursively, in terms of force fields, images, and archetypes, and so could not be read in the same way as theological language. It is just here that Lacan opens up the possibility for linking the unconscious to theological discourse. Arguing that "the unconscious is structured . . . like a language, that a material operates in it according to certain laws, which are the same laws as those discovered in the study of actual languages[1], Lacan attributes a linguistic and textual character to the unconscious itself. On this view theological texts and manifestations of the unconscious are homologous and open to common interpretive strategies. Because they are now commensurable, theological texts can be treated like the subject of a psychoanalysis, as manifesting multiple strands of meaning which become intelligible through the analytic process.

This application of Lacanian method is entirely one of my own devising. In fact, Lacan criticizes the proofs for God's existence as ways "in which, over the centuries, he has been killed off."[2] Contrary to this assessment, I shall interpret the argument as Anselm's expression of the Christian's love of God. It is not my aim to come to a decision about the proof's soundness or to decide whether the existence of God

or Anselm's conception of Him has been established, but to show how
these ends have been achieved to Anselm's satisfaction. Because I shall
treat the text like an analysand, I shall often be forced to speak of it in
a queer way, as having desires, displaying resistances, and the like.

The success of Anselm's analysis will be measured by the extent to
which the full signification of the concept of God is revealed. Succes-
sive layers of false meaning are bared through a process Anselm calls
"conceiving" (*cogitare*) when it is existentially incomplete but conceptually full and "understanding" (*intelligere*) when it culminates in existential or factual signification. A similar distinction is to be found in
Lacan's conception of the analyst's hearing (*entendre*) and understanding what is heard (*comprendre*). Although no psychoanalysis is ever
definitively closed, the proof is brought to an end when God's name is
seen through the refining of conceptualization to be nondifferent from
the way He reveals Himself to be. I shall explicate the proof by inter-
weaving logical and psychological elements just as an analysand min-
gles conscious and unconscious strands in telling his or her story. But I
shall distinguish them when necessary, bearing in mind Lacan's warn-
ing about the requirements of the double discourse, conscious and
unconscious language, "hieroglyphs inscribed simultaneously on both
sides of an obelisk, and whose meaning changes completely from one
side to the other.[3]"

A Lacanian analysis unfolds in accordance with its own lines of
force, which Lacan thinks of as truth, the truth of the patient's desire.
The patient cannot grasp the meaning of the symbols in which his
desire has become alienated. Interpretation consists in restoring to each
significant language fragment the chain of meanings from which it has
slipped, so that step by step, through the course of the analysis, a complex but coherent associative fabric of unconscious thoughts is woven
together. Anselm's proof also unfolds as a coming to consciousness of
desire, the conatus toward a God who is named at the outset against
the "voices" that obstruct the realization of desire. The proof aims to
know what is already believed as darkly present, that God exists, and
that the God whom we have named is such that He is as we have
named Him: "a-being-such-that-a-greater-cannot-be-conceived."[4] and
that he cannot be conceived as otherwise when we have thus conceived him.[5] (*Proslogion* III). For the sake of brevity I shall use such
phrases as 'God's name,' 'the divine name,' or 'Anselm's key phrase' to
denote Anselm's formulation rather than the terms 'supreme being' or
'highest being' because of conceptual difficulties connected with them
that will be considered in the final section of this paper.

Before embarking on a Lacanian reading proper, it may be useful
to notice that some presuppositions I mentioned have already become

familiar through Barth's reading of the argument. Barth claims that Anselm's concept of God breaks with the sphere of human thought. Barth thinks of this concept as God's revealed name.[6] My Lacanian reading will also attribute Anselm's key phrase to the sphere outside of conscious language, as the self-revelation of the unconscious that speaks the language of desire (in this case, God's self-revealing desire) against the text's opposing positions (the Fool's, Gaunilo's). Second, for Barth the revealed name of God is present from the start—the argument's presupposition and not its conclusion.[7] For Lacan the language of desire is present from the beginning of the analytic work but must be given the opportunity to come to expression. This means it must transcend empty speech (speech that is alienated from desire) to become full speech (speech from which the mirages of the subject have been cleared away through a recollecting of the past, in the case of the proof, the detritus of "false" images and speech). A third point of convergence lies in the future-directedness of Barth's interpretation and of Lacan's notion of full speech. For Barth, Anselm's concept of a highest being provides us with an ongoing norm for acts of thinking[9] so that it stretches out toward the future.[10] Because, for Lacan, "the effect of full speech is to reorder past contingencies by conferring on them the effect of necessities to come,"[11] a Lacanian reading must similarly conclude that Anselm's key phrase, when fully expressive of the language of desire, conveys normative force for future thought and action.

The Fool and the Divine Name: *Proslogion* II

Applied to theological texts, a Lacanian psychoanalytic interpretation has a twofold structure: first, there is the obvious level of analysis, that of the contemporary critic of the text—for example, my own role in the present essay. Second (and far less evident) is the therapeutic structure internal to the theological text itself, a *Zweifaltigkeit* inherent in the dialogical character of the argument as such. On the one hand there is the text's truth strand, the thread of desire that must be made to stand out and be supported against countervalent influences and, on the other, the level of the resistances, the positions that again and again assert themselves against the text's truth. In this section I hope to describe the argument's major strands and the linguistic strategies that are used to implement their development from a Lacanian perspective.

The structure of the argument's strands or subtexts reflects Lacan's division of psychic life into the objectifications of the subject, his alienated being as disclosed in his assumption of various roles, and the "true subject" or the unconscious that enters into language through representation by receiving a name (the son of John) or through pronomial reference. This substitution of a name for the true subject reflects a primal alienation that takes place when the subject, an absence or lack, is represented by a linguistic surrogate.

The process of alienation manifests itself in an individual's life history in what Lacan calls the mirror stage. Between the age of six months and about a year and a half the child will identify with the specular image of himself, first with another child, later with his own mirror image. The mirror stage "manifests the affective dynamism by which the subject originally identifies himself with the visual Gestalt of his own body: in relation to the still very profound lack of coordination of his own motility, it represents an ideal unity. . . ."[12] This identification of self with bodily Gestalt "situates the agency of the ego, before its social determination, in an ideal direction."[13] If the mirror stage is successfully concluded, the infant's feeling of body fragmentation is overcome and a sense of corporeal unity achieved.

But spatio-temporal wholeness is secured at the price of a narcissistic and alienated identification with an iconic or imaginary self, the ego, that henceforth will obstruct the desires of the unconscious. Unlike American ego psychologists who endorse a strengthening of the ego, Lacan believes the ego is infralinguistic and inhibits the full expression of unconscious desires through false and alienating identifications. Just as the strategies of Anselm's argument will recur over and over again, for Lacan, "this narcissistic moment in the subject is to be found in all the genetic phases of the individual, in all the degrees of human accomplishment in the person, in a before in which it must assume a libidinal frustration and an after in which it is transcended in a normative sublimation."[14]

Before proceeding to the argument proper, I shall divide it into voices or strands to facilitate a psychoanalytic account: Anselm's or the therapeutic strand representing the voice of desire through the language of God's self-revelation; the strands of the Fool and Gaunilo representing the resistances, ego ideals, and mirages of the subject; and the Painter's strand, a weak subtext of Anselm's strand, representing an early effort to extend and amplify it.

In his opening prayer Anselm asks God to help him grasp the full meaning of the divine name, "something-than-which-nothing-greater-can-be-conceived," and not, in Lacanian terms, something imaginary, an expression of the ego. Lacan calls such full understanding symbolic expression. Symbols are taken in their structuralist meaning, not as images but as signifiers, "differential elements in themselves without meaning, which acquire value only in their mutual relations."[15] Anselm's prayer is, in part, an appeal for a proof for God's existence, but mainly it pleads for the ability to express discursively the love of God that is Anselm's deepest desire.

"But can there be any such Nature," since "the Fool says in his heart, 'God is not.'" Either the Fool speaks nonsense or his denial refers to Anselm's conception of God, which he takes to be mistaken. If the latter, what belief does he offer in its stead? The full content of the Fool's foolishness emerges later, only after Anselm considers the implications of trying to imagine God as a contingent being in *Proslogion* III. In the present context we know only that God is not: there is no Other of the Fool, himself the *imago* that at this stage substitutes for the voice of Anselm's desire. The Fool, a specular image thrown forth by the unconscious to negate the language of desire that declares God to be a being such that no greater can be conceived, will now constitute in various guises an impediment to full divine self-revelation. This first discourse of the self's suppression of desire is the text's expression of the mirror stage.

A more detailed example of theological mirror-stage narcissism, one which may (retrospectively) shed light on Anselm's theological framework, is found in Descartes' account of the attributes he would confer upon himself had he the power to do so: "Now if I had existence from myself, I should have no doubts or wants, and in general nothing would be lacking in me; I should have endowed myself with all the perfections of which I have any idea—in fact I should myself be a God."[16] Sartre thinks of such a being as an "impossible synthesis" but, once posited, such a being, in Lacanian terms, can only be abandoned after the therapy is completed. In the next step of the argument, Anselm must show that God exists not only intra- but extramentally as well. Anselm introduces a new voice, that of the Painter, which now will be made to speak the language of Anselm's desire. At first, imagining what he is about to paint, the Painter has the painting only in relation to his understanding, because he has not yet painted it. Once the picture is executed, he has it in relation to his understanding, and he also understands that it exists. The Painter now substitutes for Anselm in the argument, and the painting for the divine name.

In his effort to put meaning in place of the Fool's nonsense, Anselm resorts to metaphor, a rhetorical strategy crucial to the creation of signification. It is worth noting that for Lacan "metaphor emerges at the precise point where sense emerges from nonsense."[17] Metaphor is generally defined as substituting a concrete reality for an abstract notion. For structural linguistics, metaphor is the emergence of a new meaning when one signifier, related through similarity to another, substitutes for it. By adding a psychoanalytic dimension to the structuralist view, Lacan gives metaphoricity a dynamic thrust: one of these signifiers, the one that is substituted for, falls out of the chain of signifiers, becomes latent, and leaves a space onto which a new signifying chain can be grafted.[18] The name of God has disappeared for the moment, but what has been learned from the trope of the painting may later be grafted into the interval in the signifying chain opened up by the name of God.

The purpose of the digression of the Painter is to establish that there is a disturbance in the Fool's relation to the Other, in this case to the extramental alterity of God. Anselm begins to illuminate the Fool's pathology by introducing the painting as a metaphor for the divine name. A Lacanian elaboration of the Oedipus story should shed light both on the difficulties of the Fool's position and on Anselm's effort to clarify them. In the Oedipal phase of psychosexual development, the child wishes to be everything to the mother, to substitute for what she is lacking, the phallus. The child now identifies with the symbol of this maternal desire, the phallus, which, for Lacan, is not an organic referent but "the privileged signifier of that mark in which the role of the logos is joined with the advent of desire."[19] Should the child persist in this identification with the mother, he would fail to gain entry to the symbolic realm and would become a simple extension of the mother's being.

This stage of the Oedipal phase establishes the groundplan both archetypally and in actuality for the subject's future relations to alterity. The account of the connection of the intramental painting to its actualization manifests a point-for-point structural correspondence with Lacan's description of the fusion phase of the Oedipal stage. The painting as object of the Painter's desire is experienced as different from the understanding whose object it is. Still, so long as it has merely intramental existence, it is not a painting but a lack, the substitute for another lack, the subject's desire for the extramental painting.

In his next move Anselm turns from the imagined to the actual painting, from a mental image to a fully executed object. This transition, in Lacanian terms, moves from the nonsymbolized imaginary to the symbolic realm, in this case the fully realized painting. (For Lacan the symbolic as expression, or *Auspruch*, is, like Anselm's painting, a material signifer.) This transformation of the object of desire into the truth of language first comes about through the resolution of the Oedipal conflict when the child first encounters proscription in the form of the Law of the Father. The Father proscribes the child's identification with the phallus that is desired by the mother while prohibiting the mother from reappropriating her product or returning the child to the womb. The child must give up the phallus that he is in order to have a phallus. In so doing he enters the symbolic order. The presence of the Father is attested through his law, which is speech. This law must first be recognized by the mother since, if the father's position is placed in doubt, the child remains subjected to the mother. Recognition of the Law of the Father gives the child access to the Name of the Father

(Lacan plays on the homonym *nom de père* as both name and no-saying of the Father) and with it into the world of human culture.[20] Because for Freud the Father who establishes the Law is the Father of the primal horde slain by his sons, "the symbolic Father is, insofar as he signifies this Law, [also] the dead Father."[21] This process, the recognition that the self and the object of desire are autonomous wholes, has been concluded successfully by the Painter, although he is far from giving full discursive expression to the ultimate object of desire, the divine name.

The text goes on to examine the progress made through this excursus by the Fool. Now God's name stands at least in relation to the Fool's understanding, so that he has come part of the way toward recognizing the alterity of the object (it is present to the understanding). But he has not yet understood it as actual. The Fool, still ignorant of the symbolic register in which the divine name is encoded, is trapped in incomplete alterity. Because he is unable to recognize the conceptual significance of the divine name, the object of his desire cannot be released into independent existence. Using Lacan's metaphor, the Fool refuses entry into the Name-of-the-Father because his desire is snared in the maternal womb of his own understanding. In Anselm's formulation "even the Fool is convinced that 'something than which nothing greater can be conceived' at least stands in relation to his understanding."

In logical terms, the difficulty connected with the use of the metaphor of the painting is that it substitutes something for something else that can have no substitute, a unique name, a class term whose only member is itself. But stipulating the logical conditions for the use of a unique name by supplying an example can only be misleading. The Fool has an inkling of this problem, which will later be seen to provide the occasion for Gaunilo's attempted refutation of the argument.

Necessary and Contingent Existence (*Proslogion* III)

Proslogion II concludes with a summary: when one thinks of a being such that a greater cannot be conceived, one cannot think of this being as existing in thought alone but as existing also in reality, since this is greater. It is by now a commonplace that the presupposition of this part of the proof, existence is a perfection, has been challenged by Kant's claim that existence adds nothing to the concept of the subject. (There is no more money in one hundred real dollars than there is in one hundred imaginary dollars.) But the version of the argument in *Proslogion* III does not depend on holding that existence is a property of God (on which the Kantian refutation hangs) but that *necessary* existence is such a property.

In Lacanian terms neither the mirror stage nor the first phase of the Oedipal stage has been fully transcended. This was expressed theologically in *Proslogion* II when the Fool ascribed merely conceptual existence to the divine name and failed to attribute otherness (extra-mental existence) to God. By identifying the understanding with its divine object, he remained snared in the maternal womb. The psychological impasse of *Proslogion* II is now overcome in the context of a discussion of the highest being's necessary existence as contrasted with what is entailed by attributing contingent existence to Him. In this section I hope to relate the difference between necessary and contingent existence to the required condition for accession to the Name of the Father: the child's acceptance of lack in the form of symbolic castration as the price for admission into language and culture.

A preliminary sketch of this particularly dense part of Anselm's argument and its psychological corollaries may be useful. The argument falls into two parts.[22] First, the hypothesis is posited that, if God exists, he exists as a contingent being. This hypothesis leads to the conclusion that the existence of God is impossible. The psychological outcome can, in Lacanian terms, be expressed as despair and anguish when the deepest desires of the unconscious—in the present instance, Anselm's desire for God—are thwarted. The second part of *Proslogion* III considers the hypothesis that God exists necessarily. If true, Anselm's desires are realized and the "true" subject can enter unreservedly into pure joy and bliss. Such a psychological outcome cannot be fully realized, but this can only become apparent later in the dialogue with Gaunilo.

In the first part of the present section of the argument, its full implications (following Malcolm) are best grasped by considering first what follows from positively affirming his nonexistence. If God, a being than which none greater can be conceived, does not exist, then He cannot come into existence. If He did, He would merely have happened to come into existence (an impossible contention) or his existence would have been caused by some other thing. In either case He would be a limited being. In Anselm's terms, "the creature would rise above the Creator." Instead of God's being an autonomous being, He would be dependent upon another for his existence. But, by our conception of Him, this is clearly impossible. The crucial point for a psychoanalytic development of the argument follows from this: since He cannot come into existence for the reasons given, and if He does not exist, his existence is impossible.

A Lacanian investigation of this possibility is parasitic on one of the most complex articles in the *Ecrits*, "The Subversion of the Subject and the Dialectic of Desire in the Freudian Unconscious."[23] We saw earlier that the relationship between the subject and the unconscious is mediated by the Law of the Father and the failure to transcend the identification with maternal desire that ensues when the process that orders these relations remains incomplete. If the child remains bound to the mother as the source of fulfillment, he is doomed to disappointment, for even if the mother tries to satisfy all his needs, she cannot hope to fulfill his absolute demand for absolute love. Demand transcends the capacity to satisfy need. It is in this gap (*béance*) between need and demand that desire is born. Lacan distinguishes need, a biological force; lack, an irreversible incompleteness; and desire, a conatus "which begins to take shape in the margin in which demand [a request for love] becomes separated from need."[24] But because demand is always demand of the Other, it remains at the mercy of the Other's whim, giving rise to the phantom of the Other's omnipotence.

But man does not know his own desire because the unconscious is the discourse of the Other. Lacan means this in two senses: first, "the *de* is to be understood in the sense of the Latin *de* (objective determination)," discourse from the Other, and, second "the *de* provides what grammarians call the 'subjective determination', namely that it is *qua* Other that he desires, which is what provides the true compass of human passion."[25] This is why the analyst does not try to meet the analysand's demands but speaks in the voice of the Other and asks, " 'What do you want [*che vuoi*]?' "[26] The double meaning attributed to the Other is tied to the inevitability of human frustration and anguish. Just as the maternal Other cannot hope to realize the child's absolute demands for perfection, so too access is barred to the fullness of the Other that is the object of unconscious desires. (This Other is written as Ø, barred O). If the Other as the "locus of truth," and the "treasure of the signifier" is, as Lacan claims, grounded in lack, the relations to alterity can only end in despair. The "signifier of a lack in the Other," what Lacan calls the signifier of the barred Other, S(Ø), is inherent in the Other's function as "the treasure of the signifier."[27]

This account of the Other provides an entering wedge for understanding the opening section of *Proslogion* III in Lacanian terms. We saw that the Other is "the treasure of the signifier" but cannot itself enter into plenary presence. At the same time, "the Other is required (*che vuoi*) to respond to the value of this treasure,"[28] from its own place, that is, it must say what it wants by entering the chain of signification. It can do so either from a buried chain of signifiers, or by breaching another (upper) chain of signifiers. The Other is required to respond because, in a point of cardinal importance for Anselm's argument, Lacan insists "*There is no Other than the Other.*"[29] Lacan intends this reply in a psychoanalytic and not a theological sense. But, in the context of the ontological argument, Lacan's point that "there is no Other than the Other" should be taken at face value. It is now possible to picture in Lacanian terms the psychoanalytic equivalent of hypothesizing God's nonexistence (as based on the contradictory conception of Him as a contingent being): the Other exists only as a lack.

The anguish of this position can be understood in terms of the relation among signifiers. A signifier is defined as that which represents the subject for another signifier. As such this signifier is "the signifier for which all the other signifiers represent the subject: that is to say in the absence of this signifier, all the other signifiers represent nothing."[30] The subject is an absence in the set of signifiers and, as such, inexpressible. (It can be represented as a negative number (-1) and its utterances, whose form is derived through a complex process that need not be replicated here, expressed as $\sqrt{-1}$, an irrational number.[31]) In sum, the statements of the unconscious are never directly accessible. It can therefore be argued that the Fool's earlier formulation, "God is not," is the unfortunate result of trying to transcribe unconscious content, God's plenary presence, directly, a procedure that has just been shown to be impossible. In the present context (examining the hypothesized nonexistence of God), anguish is experienced first as the result of recognizing that the subject is founded on a nullity; second, that there is no Other of this nullity; and finally, that the individual, thrown into the abyss of his own nonbeing, can only think the existence of God as impossible.

The next step in Anselm's argument considers the alternative hypothesis of God's necessary existence. If God does exist, nothing can have caused his existence nor can he "just happen to cease to exist. So if he exists, his existence is necessary." This conclusion is reached by Lacan by an altogether different route. After speculating on the signifier as founded in lack, Lacan's comments take a remarkably Christian turn. Explicitly rejecting the possibility of rational proof for the existence of God, Lacan suggests the solution that the Christian kerygma proclaims for establishing the existence of the Other: loving him.[32]

An alternative account for expressing the subject is also given in a dark Lacanian utterance. To the question "What am I?" Lacan replies: "I am in the place from which a voice is heard clamoring, 'The universe is a defect in the purity of Non-Being.' "[33] This oracular pronouncement can be taken to mean that the subject "fades" or withdraws from his discourse. Once outside of language, he cannot know whether he is alive or dead and thus can be said to undergo a kind of death. "This place, is called *jouissance* [a term linked to rights and to sexual enjoyment, in this context, boundless and impossible bliss], and it is the absence of this that makes the universe vain."[34] The gap opened by this analysis parallels in point-for-point fashion the situation explicated in *Proslogion* III. When the I is seen as grounded in lack, a nullity in a chain of signifiers that must, but cannot, be brought into language because these signifiers represent nothing, then God is impossible. But if we begin with the fact that there is speech, even if the chain of signifiers is grounded in nullity, this nullity may be ontologically understood in some alternative fashion. When the I retreats — in theological language, "dies to itself" — or when, in Lacanian terms, "the subject fades," the Non-Being of the Other, discursively formulable only in negative terms, may actually be something boundless, inexpressible, *jouissance* without limit. But, if it is necessary that some such fathomless ground exist, still, as Lacan shows, access to it is barred.

This may be why, at the end of *Proslogion* III, the Fool continues to say in his heart: "God is not," although it has been established that "God exists supremely above all things." After the entire argument concerning God's necessary extramental existence has been traversed, the foolishness of the Fool persists. Even if it is *necessary* that there be *jouissance*, he knows he cannot experience it. The diagnosis offered in Anselm's theological terms was already stipulated in *Proslogion* II: a thing is conceived in one way when the word signifying it is thought and in another way when the very thing itself is understood. When hearing the word God it is possible to give the word no meaning or an alien meaning. While some difficulties have been overcome, access to the divine name is barred and merely verbal signification attributed to it.

The Fool's Last Stand: The Most Perfect Island

The resistances of the Fool have crystalized in the argument anticipated in the metaphor of the painting. Gaunilo, a monk of Marmoutier speaking on behalf of the Fool, contends that the distinction between merely verbal conception and genuine understanding, which guarantees the existence of the thing conceived, is an artificial one. They are in fact the same: both are verbal and verbal existence cannot be translated into actual existence.

To show this, Gaunilo in chapter 3 of *On Behalf of the Fool* first objects that the earlier analogy of the painting is misleading because the painting is an object created in time: "The picture exists first in the mind of the painter, and afterward in his work." The analogy is stretched to the breaking point if it is argued (as Anselm would be forced to do if the analogy were to hold point-for-point) that, as in the case of God, the nonexistence of the painting is inconceivable. In sum, Gaunilo contends in chapter 4, "I can conceive [of some object such as a painting] according to a fact that is real and familiar to me: but of God or a being greater than all others, I could not conceive at all, except merely according to the word." This formulation will turn out to be a fatal admission for Gaunilo and will enable Anselm, in both Lacanian and conventional theological terms, to bring the argument to the desired conclusion.

In his initial reply Gaunilo does not deny that a being such that a greater cannot be conceived can exist in the understanding but rather that from this it follows that such a being exists in reality. In chapter 6 he offers a new analogy, that of a most perfect island, a better comparison than the painting because, as the best of its kind, it can claim greater structural affinity with a highest being. But the island's existence in actuality still cannot be proved from its assumption in hypothesis.

> [Because of] the impossibility of discovering what does not exist [it] is called the lost island . . . . Now if someone should tell me that there is such an island, I should easliy understand his words, in which there is no difficulty. But, suppose that he went on to say, as if by a logical inference: '. . . [This island exists in the understanding but] it is more excellent not to be in the understanding alone, but to exist both in the understanding and in reality, for this reason it must exist. For if it does not exist, any land which really exists is more excellent than it; and so the island already understood by you to be more excellent will not be more excellent.[35]

Gaunilo contends such a proof must be a jest since unreal objects are conceivable without necessarily existing in reality. But in Lacanian terms, Gaunilo makes real progress when the fantasy object, a most perfect island, substitutes for the divine name and thereby advances beyond the limitations of the painting. The success of the therapy will depend on full recognition of the difference between *all* other objects and the divine name to which alone the logic of his argument pertains.

A distinction must be made before the argument's final step and the therapy can be successfully concluded: the difference between conceiving and understanding. For Anselm, understanding is the faculty that grasps factual existence while the faculty of conceiving comprehends whatever is intelligible. Were the existence of God a matter for the understanding, Gaunilo could argue that *any* existing thing can not be understood not to exist once it is known that the object *in fact* exists. In the case of conceiving, we can conceive of many things that exist as nonexisting, even when we know that factually they exist. So, objects other than God cannot be understood as nonexisting when they are known to exist, because they can, in fact, be imagined not to exist. But it is self-contradictory to say that a being such that a greater cannot be conceived can be conceived not to exist.

While from a Lacanian perspective both conceiving and under-standing would be interpreted as conscious processes, manifestations of the unconscious slip into conceiving since understanding purports to deal with factual existents rather than the facts of desire. Lacan grants that the perception of factual existents (roughly equivalent to Anselm's "understanding") can be allocated to the ego as "the seat of perceptions ... [and that it] reflects the essence of the objects it perceives."[36] But in doing so it fails to reflect its own unconscious affec-tations. But there are objects, the ego itself for example, that can become "a means of the speech addressed to you from the unconscious, a weapon to resist its recognition ... fragmented in that it bears speech, and whole in that it helps in not hearing it."[37] Such an object both brings the symptoms clearly to view and turns the subject away from them. It is this contact with the "signifying material of his symptoms" that becomes possible at the level Anselm calls conceiving and that we are to search for in the meaning of the signifier, "most perfect island."

Access to this signifying material can be gained through a funda-mental concept of Lacan's psychoanalytical epistemology, the *objet petit a* (the *a* standing for autre). Earlier I suggested that the unconscious is struc-tured as a nexus of signifiers that successively alienate and channel pri-mordial desire. This path of "lures and alienation" is marked by changing objects until at last desire becomes reflexive and ends up as the desire of another desire. This process of substitution is interpreted narrowly in terms of its genesis in individual life history and broadly as a law of psy-chic life. In the first and narrower sense the lost object is what the subject wishes to be in its initial split from the mother, the phallus for the mother. The narrow sense also includes part objects (such as the breast) substituted by the instincts to fill in the fissure that now separates the child from his desired object. Second, in a broader sense the *objet petit a* designates any signifier or representative of the object of lack when it is deprived of its symbolic referent, the phallus.[38] But, as Lemaire points out, "Every object of desire, every object of alienating identification will reveal itself to be ephemeral and destined to be supplanted because it is incapable of stopping up the lack inscribed in the subject from the start by the very fact of his being eclipsed in the signifier."[39]

The most perfect island described by Gaunilo is a signifier that structurally replicates the object that has fallen from the significative chain and, as such, is an *objet petit a*. It cannot fill the fissure between the primordial object of desire and present demand but it carries out a secondary function, one already envisioned by Lacan in another connection: the island serves (as Lacan says in a moment of theological reflection when speaking of religious icons or images) "as a go-between with the divinity."[40] (1981:113).

A single step remains for Anselm to reveal fully the ontic status of the island as an *objet petit a*. The relation between the Law of the Father and *jouissance* provides the psychological underpinning for Anselm's response to the most-perfect-island thesis. Anselm's rebuttal is based on a key distinction referred to earlier, that between a being greater than all others and a being than which no greater can be conceived. In Lacanian terms, *jouissance* is encoded in the divine name, which is, for Anselm, throughout the course of the argument "a-being such-that-a-greater-cannot-be-conceived." This name is not to be confused with another, "a being greater than all other beings." Anselm's entire therapy, which only now can expose their distinctiveness, depended on this difference all along. The two concepts, although not alike, are easy to confuse and lead to the unconscious misprisions of the Fool and Gaunilo. Now Anselm shows that a being greater than all other beings is a misleading verbal representation of God leading to false conclusions about His nature. It is a designation founded on a lack: a greater being than the deficient highest being can be imagined, one than which a greater cannot even be conceived. Unlike Anselm's God, "greatest being" lacks conceptual and ontic fullness.

May it then be assumed that, once this difference is grasped, admission can be gained to a plenum without lack symbolized by the correct name of God? By no means. The previous analysis has shown that conceptualization of the divine name rests on *difference*: the difference between a highest being and a-being-such-that-a-greater-cannot-be-conceived, and difference is itself grounded in negation and lack. Does the hope for reaching into the ground of *jouissance* inevitably lead to the lure and seduction of mirage-like substitutions? Lacan shows that although direct access to *jouissance* is barred, it can, through the phallic signifier, be reached in a restricted way. The elusiveness of *jouissance* is not the result of "a bad arrangement of society" nor of some lack in the Other (as if the Other existed), nor of 'original sin,' a myth used to explain this exclusion."[41] Instead it is to be accounted for by the necessity for the subject's entry into language and culture. But in the economy of desire, such accession to symbolization demands a price: sacrificial castration. Because its castration can be imaged, the phallus as image is a natural locus for prohibition, for the curtailment of *jouissance*.[42] Only by excision of the imaginary phallus, barring it from the plenitude of *jouissance*, can the phallus as signifier or symbol come into being.

When this interpretation is applied to Anselm's argument, Gaunilo's therapy and that of the Fool are brought to closure. Both have come to understand that if the paternal law has been interiorized, then the fulfillment of primordial desire is barred. Denied direct access to *jouissance*, they can only hear the divine name in its conceptual fullness as a master signifier. In a succinct formula strikingly pertinent to the phase of Anselm's argument just considered, Lacan writes: "Indeed the law seems to be giving the order, '*Jouis* [have *jouissance*]!' to which the subject can only reply, '*Jouis*' [I hear], *the jouissance being no more than understood*" (emphasis is mine).[43]

Notes

1. Jacques Lacan, *Ecrits: A Selection*, trans. Alan Sheridan (New York: W.W. Norton, 1977), 234.

2. Ibid., 317.

3. Anika Lemaire, *Jacques Lacan*, trans. David Macey (London: Routledge and Kegan Paul, 1977), 250.

4. St. Anselm of Canterbury, *Proslogion* II, from "St. Anselm," in *The Ontological Argument: From St. Anselm to Contemporary Philosophers*, ed. Alvin Plantinga (New York: Anchor Books, Doubleday and Company, 1965)

5. Ibid., *Proslogion* III.

6. Karl Barth, *Anselm: Fides Quarens Intellectum* (Richmond, Va.: John Knox Press, 1958), 73.

7. Ibid.

8. Jacques Lacan, "The Function of Language in Psychoanalysis," in *Speech and Language in Psychoanalysis*, ed. and trans. Anthony Wilden (Baltimore: Johns Hopkins University Press, 1968), 18; Lacan, *Ecrits*, 45.; John P. Muller and William J. Richardson, *Lacan and Language: A Reader's Guide to Ecrits* (New York: International Universities Press, 1982), 70.

9. Arthur C. McGill, "Karl Barth: A Presupposition of the Proof: The Name of God," in *The Many-faced Argument*, ed. John H. Hick and Arthur C. McGill (New York: Macmillan Company, 1967), 97-98.

10. Barth, *Anselm*, 171.

11. Lacan, "Function of Language," 72.

12. Lacan, *Ecrits*, 18-19.

13. Ibid., 18.

14. Ibid., 24.

15. Ibid., ix.

16. Rene Descartes, "Meditations on First Philosophy," in *Philosophical Writings*, ed. and trans. Elizabeth Anscombe and Peter Thomas Geach (Indianapolis, Ind.: Bobbs-Merrill Company, 1971), 87.

17. Lacan, *Ecrits*, 158.

18. Lemaire, *Jacques Lacan*, 197.

19. Lacan, *Ecrits*, 287.

20. Ibid., 196-98.

21. Ibid., 198.

22. Norman Malcolm, "Anselm's Ontological Arguments," in Hick and McGill, *The Many-Faced Argument*, 308-310.

23. Lacan, *Ecrits*, 292-325.

24. Ibid., 311.

25. Ibid., 312.

26. Ibid.

27. Ibid., 316.

28. Ibid.

29. Ibid.

30. Ibid.

31. Ibid., 317.

32. Ibid.

33. Ibid.

34. Ibid.

35. Ibid., 11.

36. Lacan, *Ecrits*, 134.

37. Ibid., 137.

38. Lemaire, *Jacques Lacan*, 174.

39. Ibid.

40. Jacques Lacan, *The Four Fundamental Concepts of Psychoanalysis*, ed. Jacques-Alain Miller, trans. Alan Sheridan (New York: W.W. Norton and Company), 113.

41. Lacan, *Ecrits*, 317.

42. Ibid., 319.

43. Ibid.

Works Cited

Anselm of Canterbury, St. In *The Ontological Argument: From St. Anselm to Contemporary Philosophers*. Ed. Alvin Plantinga, New York: Anchor Books, Doubleday and Company, 1965.

Barth, Karl. *Anselm: Fides Quarens Intellectum*. Richmond, Va.: John Knox Press, 1958.

Descartes, Rene. "Meditations on First Philosophy." In *Philosophical Writings*. Ed. and trans. Elizabeth Anscombe and Peter Thomas Geach. Indianapolis, In.: Bobbs-Merrill Company, 1971.

Lacan, Jacques. "The Function of Language in Psychoanalysis." In *Speech and Language in Psychoanalysis*. Ed. and trans. Anthony Wilden. Baltimore: Johns Hopkins University Press, 1968.

_____. *Ecrits: A Selection*. Trans. Alan Sheridan. New York: W.W. Norton and Company, 1977.

_____. *The Four Fundamental Concepts of Psychoanalysis*. Ed. Jacques-Alain Miller, trans. Alan Sheridan. New York: W.W. Norton and Company, 1981.

Lemaire, Anika. *Jacques Lacan*. Trans. David Macey. London: Routledge and Kegan Paul, 1977.

Malcolm, Norman. "Anselm's Ontological Arguments." In *The Many-Faced Argument*. Ed. John H. Hick and Arthur C. McGill. New York: Macmillan Publishing Company, 1967.

McGill, Arthur C. "Karl Barth: A Presupposition of the Proof: The Name of God." In *The Many-Faced Argument*, 1967.

Muller, John P. and William J. Richardson. *Lacan and Language: A Reader's Guide to Ecrits*. New York: International Universities Press, 1982.

Summary

David Crownfield

One simply cannot do what Edith Wyschogrod sets out to do in this essay! What is more, she knows it. To treat the dialogue of Anselm and Boso as a psychoanalytic dialogue! To attempt a Lacanian psychoanalysis of a text where there is no conversation, no transference, no possibility of the emergence of new speech in the text as a result of the analysis!

Hers is a calculated transgression, "good for nothing," as she says of Lacan. By this violation of academic propriety she intends to make something interesting (perhaps even useful) happen. In the course of it, she attributes to various features of Lacan's discourse meanings I don't see there; she asserts intentions and functions to the participants in the dialogue that cannot be justified in the text; she invents a therapeutic agenda for the argument, a psychoanalytic meaning to the question of the existence of God, that are flat counter to the customary constraints in such matters. And she does, indeed, make something interesting and useful (perhaps even important) happen.

This impossible project is conceivable on the surprising but legitimate ground that Lacan's recognition of the linguistic and textual structure of the unconscious establishes a homology, a commensurability between theological texts and manifestations of the unconscious. (But her statement that texts can thus be treated "like the subject of a psychoanalysis" perhaps goes too far, in view of the extraordinary complexities, discontinuities, eccentricities of the Lacanian subject. As the text is not a body of suffering or of *jouissance*, its subject is a simply linguistic subject, unlike the introjective, fractally linguistic subject Lacan speaks of.)

Anselm's proof of God's existence, says Wyschogrod, is to be read as the Christian's love of God. Through refinement of conceptualization God's name is to be seen as nondifferent from the way He reveals Himself to be. (The analogy with Karl Barth's treatment of Anselm is

115

pertinent, not only in its construing the argument as presupposing the Name of God, but also in its recognition of the temporal and ultimately future-directed import of the argument.) This Name is at the same time the language of desire, the self-revelation of the unconscious; it is the love of God that is Anselm's deepest desire. Wyschogrod correlates this with Lacan's observations on love in psychoanalysis: "I can only just prove to the Other that he exists, not with the proofs for the existence of God, ... but by loving him." (In Lacan, this is the thought of the analysand, unable to know that he is alive as a subject, displacing this problem from his own lack of being to the love in which he guarantees for himself the being of the analyst: the transference.)

Love, in psychoanalysis, is customarily dealt with in the context of idealization and identification. For Lacan, this is tied up with the principle that desire is desire of the other's desire, the desire to be real as mirrored in the Other. Transference is the focusing of this process on the analyst as the signifier of the Other. Lacan rejects equation of the Other with God; is God then another signifier of the Other? Is the love of God a transference love, a signification of desire, a quest for my reflection in the ultimate mirror? Wyschogrod does not discuss these questions directly, but her treatment of Anselm necessarily raises them.

Her treatment of the question of the Other has a number of interesting features. We speak here, of course, of the grand Other, contrasted always in Lacan with the various specific others, objects of desire, signifiers of lack and of imagined fulfilment, that Lacan calls *objet petit a*, objects with a small a (*a* for *autre*, other) — part objects and cathected objects. The Fool who says in his heart that there is no God has a pathology of relation to the Other: lacking an Other to the nullity of existence, he is lost in the abyss of his own nonbeing. At one point, Wyschogrod speaks of the "extramental alterity of God," which almost makes God an object *petit a*. Yet one of the strengths of her paper is the clarification of how the painting Anselm uses as an illustration, or the most perfect island, or even the merely mental existence of God are inadequate precisely because they reduce the Other to a petit other.

Descartes, she says, situates his proof for God in a context of mirror-stage narcissism, the fantasy of a subject that is complete, capable of giving itself all perfections, itself a God. Failing such a self-mirroring, I must, Descartes holds, believe in a perfect being. Such a formulation, obviously, gives us a being of specular integrity and imagined omnipotence, a highest object *petit a*, rather than the Other. The critical issue, and the point on which I feel Wyschogrod is most original and most helpful, is how this is distinguished from what Anselm is doing.

Lacan never tells us what he means by the Other. There are times when the Other takes the form of Mother ("desire is desire of the

Other"). The inescapable bar imposed by the Law of the Father against fusion with mother has a Real otherness about it; it is, in a sense, the voice of the Other. (But there is no Other of the Other; so it is not a question of a conflict of Others.) The language of the unconscious is the voice of the Other (both in the sense that the other's perceived desires, demands, and prohibitions speak in the return of the repressed, and in the sense that the unconscious is itself other to consciousness, to ego, to what I suppose "I" am). We have just seen the analyst as Other; Wyschogrod reads God as Other. In language, the Other is split, barred, unattainable, signified by the various objects *a*: the enigma of the Other corresponds to the incoherence of the self, is displaced and masked and misconceived in the symbolic play of signification.

For Lacan, the Other is not to be read as God. For Wyschogrod, God is to be read as the Other. How is this possible? It is not that Lacan means the Other to signify Mother, or Father, or the unconscious; it is rather that mother, and father, and the otherness of myself to myself, are signifiers of the Other: of the Real as necessity, of *jouissance* (orgasm, ecstasy, immediacy of life—chronically barred and displaced), of death. Lacan's refusal to identify God as the Other is related to his conviction that God is an objectification, a fantasy signifier of the Other, another object *petit a*. Only if God can be shown to signify, or be, the Other in some way not reducible to such objectification and distortion could the equation be sustained.

But this is exactly what Anselm, as read by Wyschogrod, is about. "That than which no greater can be conceived"—that which exceeds, transgresses, surpasses the conception and signification by which it is invoked, that which differs from every painting, perfect island, or even conceptualized god precisely in that it exceeds the conceptualization, the representation, the signification. It is other to the whole structure of signification-by-opposition; it is indeed the Other necessary for signification to occur at all (necessary not as a referent, but as the Real). As such, it is the exception, the conception of which requires its existence, because it is the conception that there is Other, that there is that which exceeds conceptual existence and the displaced world of objects *petit a*. Even so, it is not the cognitive comprehension of this intentionality of conceptualization that is conclusive; it is the telos of desire in the love of God, the love of the Other—in the world, in practice, as well as in discourse—that is the affirmation of the necessary existence of God.

Wyschogrod sharpens the argument by correlating the theological distinction between necessary and contingent existence with the contrast between the unattainable Other and the lack, the castration, acceptance of which is necessary to enter into the world of language

and culture. Castration is the mark, the symbol, of finitude and contingency. We should note that Wyschogrod does not, as Scott finds
Lacan suggesting, hold that subjection to a master Identity is necessary,
but rather that the acknowledgment of finitude and lack is the entry-
way to social existence. The relation of finite existence to the Other is
not subjection, but the love of God.

There are two, mutually reflecting, problems with Wyschogrod's
whole argument. Desire, as we have repeatedly seen in these essays, is
illusion, it is the excess of demand over need, it is the impossible desire
to be mirrored and secured in the other's desire. How can we make the
passage from empty desire to the love of God anything but the projection of our illusion into the heavens? And how, on the other side, does
the concept of God, with the images, traditions and practices through
which it has acquired its place in the language, the discursive practices
in which we embed it, continue to escape entrapment in the objects
petit a?

The second of these questions is almost the opposite of what I
asked in response to Charles Winquist's essay. I wanted Winquist to
explicate in what sense his open, unconstrained discourse was to be
called theological, and to show where it connected with the familiar
contexts of the term. Wyschogrod has made that connection, and I am
pointing out its dangers. (There are, of course, always dangers; both
Anselmian argument and iconoclastic interrogation are disciplined trac-
ings of them.)

It is the first of my two questions to Wyschogrod, the passage from
empty desire to love of God, that marks the point where I have most
difficulty with her argument. I am inclined to think, though, that it is
in the analysis of texts, traditions, signifying practices, that the role of
desire—and if it is possible the surpassing of desire, in the love of
God—might become intelligible or signifiable.

6.

God and the Utopianism of Language

Gabriel Vahanian

By Way of Prolegomena

Voice is a way of being, argues Giorgio Agamben,[1] as though the statement could not be reversed: being is a way of speaking. And yet it is the same author who also points out that "the appearance of a new religion always coincides with a new revelation of language and a new religion means above all a new experience of language."[2] So much so, indeed, that in order for God to be, there must—also—be language (wherein *yes* is *yes* and *no* is *no* at one and the same time as is the *yes* to God at one and the same time a *no* to the idol). There is no religion unless God is tipped into language, or else he is frozen into an idol. Being God, God can only be without being. (Dieu ne peut qu'être sans l'être.) Not this or that, he is *verbum:* Verb is the word. Yet a word not contained by any language.

Indeed, language *contains* no word or else it is a dead language, at best a topic of language.

Like a map, language is no *topos:* it is *outopos,* and for that reason man always lies beyond man as does the ideal or imaginary—at their juncture, where experience is experience of a new thing, a new world, a new life. Through the Word, that is, ultimately, through language, man, being both sinful and justified, is that which he is not and is not that which he is. He speaks.

To speak is to have faith. Hemmed in by no language, man is much less hemmed in by the world. Not that he can change the world even as, through faith, his life can be changed. Tradition calls this a conversion. But conversion without the reconversion of one's life and of one's world is not enough. Without an eschatology, salvation turns into withdrawal and escape from the world, pie in the sky or gnosis. And that is a denial of that religious dimension par excellence of language, evinced by what I call its utopianism.

A fact means nothing. Meaning occurs not because things are *per se* meaningful but in spite of their meaninglessness; grace abounds in spite of sin.

Likewise, speaking is not merely saying. Nor is it merely doing. It *means*. It signifies. But speaking is signified as much as it signifies. It is textured in signification. And signification is no classification of do's and don't's, of gods and idols. Just as it could be said that language is iconoclastic if only because it is symbolic, so also it must be said that a sign points less beyond itself than to the subversion of the signified through the signifier as well as of the signifier through the signified.

If words are symbols or even icons, signs are by contrast only words. And what counts is indeed the word, not the name (with or without capital initials).

The word: that is, a bridge across language as though across a bankless river.

Was there ever a word that was not the rival of another? Its contrary? Its simile? "I love you. Neither do I?" *Sacrificium intellectus:* a word leaping onto another to grasp or be grasped by it; or image: of identity at the cost of difference, at the cost of identity.

Identity and difference. The One and the Many. The Same and the Other. As many words as seek only to hem the word in by tracing it back to a place where it could not find place—the body—or by reducing it to a soundless body. Words that rival one another and would hem language in by pretending to lead the way, and bank in the river. Words that, rivaling one another, are therefore waylaid. Words astray that cause us to stray away from being or, rather, from that verbal condition of ours so long as, for the time being, we are what we are not and are not what we are. Only the speechless are frustrated.

The same holds for the classic opposition of faith and reason. Two rivers in the same bed. Like body and soul. Or like God and man. Time and again, tradition, pinning itself down, takes the word for what it means, and wants to go beyond. Beyond the word. Into metaphysics, a sort of premature structuralism for which the soul and the body, God and man, are opposed to one another, lost as they are one in the other. God in man, the soul in the body. The signified in the signifier. Lost, or raptured on by the other. Named one by the other. Though without either's being called into question. Into speech.

The reason that moves mountains is itself nontransferable. Whether reason leads to God, or is reasonable whether it leads to God or to the devil, matters little: it trades on meaning by swapping signs. Yet without signi-fying, like words that lack the word.

To signify: not to be moored so much as to be anchored. Not pinned down so much as penned in. Written out. As is that very word of God for which God — neither signifier nor signified — is nothing but a word, *l'autre de l'autre*.

A word like other words. At least so far as the dictionary is concerned. Or, for that matter, language itself. A noun even. Yet at once proper and common. That which, being no place, can only take place, and takes place only to the extent that it does not replace language — much less the utopianism of the speech thereof when it breaks into words, into a "logic"; that is, an instance at once of revelation and of reason. Of revelation, should reason not shy away from it by reasoning itself out. Of reason, should revelation not sink into revelation.

Reason and revelation: two languages, one and the same logic, one and the same bed — the logos.

Logos: neither being nor nonbeing, those twin topics of a logocentrism held apart by reasons rather than together by reason.

Logos: that is, utopianism of language rather than its sublimation or its concatenation of words into sound and fury. Tipping the body into speech as well as space into time: the timeliness of eternity.

Hence the problem: Not time and being, much less being and nonbeing, or even time and difference. But time and language. *As* language.

Time: "une parole qui dure" (Maurice Leenhardt) — a word that lasts yet without outlasting itself. And lasts, not so much because as in spite of either the nature of language or its structure: by reason of the utopianism of language, that is, of the fact that language only occurs when and where it is without precedent. I mean, by reason of that utopianism that is not to be reduced to that of nature (metaphysics)or to that of history (structuralism). That is, to that of an apocalypse as the end of time, as though coming from beyond time. Or, for that matter, from beyond language. As though anything could separate us from the Word become flesh — once and for all. Language has no more precedent than does creation or the fullness of time.

Psalm 116:10 (II Corinthians 4:13): "I believed, and so I spoke." Lacan: ". . . d'ecrit j'ai plus que je n'écrois."

Safouan: "La barre qui figure dans le schéma du signe représente bien une union: seulement, ce n'est pas cette union du signifiant et du signifié qui en est le principe, mais, comme le disait Lacan, leur séparation. Non pas au sens spatial de l'existence parallèle, de chaque côté de la barre, d'un signifiant et d'un signifié. Bien plutôt, ce dernier doit-il advenir et ce que la barre représente, c'est ce qui, avec le signifiant se profile tant comme appel comme résistance au signifié: une barre à franchir."[3]

The argument: Though language is a technique, technique is itself the price of language. Hence, there is no technique outside language, which of course makes sense if the distinction between technique as tool and as method still holds (the former, like a hammer, extends man; the latter affects him within as well as without, even alters him). Technique is thus a metaphor of language rather than that language, serving as a tool, is analagous to technique: God is word, reality is verbal, and verbal is also the human condition. On this view, analogy belongs with the sacred; metaphor with utopia, the sole horizon of which is language (whether about God or about man), just as the sole horizon of both God and man is the Christ.

Language at the Price of Technique

Outside Language No Technique

Whatever its origin — natural or divine — no one ever seems to have fully ignored that language hides a technique.

Better still, no one seems to have ever doubted that, besides consisting of a technique, and in contrast to every other technique that tends to depersonalize or dehumanize, language cancels itself out whenever it departs from its task of personalizing man as well as of humanizing society.

Again, by contrast with technics in general, which are, so to speak, cumulative and owe their efficiency to their further rationalization or standardization, language is really and exclusively a treasure, I mean, a thesaurus: not being cumulative, paradoxically it owes its sole efficiency to the fact that it resists or escapes rationalization. And yet rationalization is only possible through language and works only insofar as it works through language, insofar as language steers clear of its own rationalization. Language is the price — at the price of technique. Not one, at least, to which all other techniques are in debt regardless of their respective achievements. Or, rather, precisely because of their achievements which, as so many "words, words, words," are ultimately put into question by or tested against language. Language is efficient insofar as it is a technique. But efficiency alone is not a sufficient justification of technique. Without language, outside language there is no technique. As Chomsky points out, although we use language in order to communicate, communication itself is a secondary function of language. Grammar and the efficiency of communication are two different things.[4]

Through language, everything can be brought to reason. The least sound, the most furtive gesture, they can all be rationalized. Language even requires it. To wit, George Orwell's counter utopia, *1984*, where language finally is itself to be given up to the highest conceivable degree of rationalization under the cover of Newspeak. As if to show that, if there be any utopia, it must require the excision of language — unless, of course, exactly the opposite is what is being shown! Namely, that utopia can never result from some rationalization or another, much less if as in Newspeak language is itself, in the process, being elided, ablated, at the price ultimately of a newfangled *sacrificium intellectus* — that of language. Of the word in the words, of the word with the words, of the word under the words.

Not that utopia is a matter of words alone, whether those of classi- fication or of nomenclature, those distant echoes of some primordial word claiming itself as *arche*, the *sine qua non* of order. In utopia, order is *an-archic*. As is, indeed, grammar itself. And grammar is to language as creation is to nature, destiny (or redemption) to history, and pleroma to gnosis or life after death. Or, for that matter, revelation to reason. And Word to words. In the Newspeak of *1984*, language is reduced to words. Forgotten is the fact that language is the condition of the reason only because it is also the condition of faith. Language does not opt between faith and reason, nor does it lie beyond or outside of them. And no more than a poem can lie outside language, can utopia occur without language, through Newspeak alone, unless it is a counterfeit. Either language is the horizon of utopia or else speaking in tongues and Newspeak are the alternatives. Just as, being the condition of rea- son, language cannot be corrected by reason,[5] and just as language, the condition of faith, cannot be replaced with glossolalia, so also can no utopia lie in words alone, that is, in the perversion of language. No utopia is worth realizing unless it can and must be subverted by lan- guage. Which language, being symbolic, is by the same token iconoclas- tic. A technique.

Analogy and Metaphor: The Verbal Condition of Man

Language is a technique; I follow Gadamer in pointing out that Aris- totle himself had already said so when he defined man as being endowed with logos, as one who reasons. He reasons, however, on the grounds as well as to the extent of a language whose *techne* consists in distinguishing the useful from the useless: put differently, in anticipat- ing the future — anticipating it rather than "fulfilling" it by anticipation if not by proxy.

Language is a technique. But, then, how comes it that, especially if we have known it all along, we should have waited so long — M. Safouan wonders — for linguistics to see the light of day? How is it that, more im- portant, neither the philosophical nor the theological tradition of the West has focused on the implication, namely, the verbal condition of man?

In spite of Scriptures and the Word of God; in spite of various stories such as creation and the Tower of Babel, the Word become flesh and Pentecost; in spite of revelation, how is it that the discourse of faith bequeathed by tradition has actually served to avoid if not to cancel the evidence of language, of linguistics?

For his part, Gadamer answers that question by saying: "it was the religious tradition of the West that hindered serious thought about language." Perhaps.

But, then, what kind of religious tradition?

Obviously, I think, a religious tradition still caught up in the meshes of myth. Entirely geared to the sacred. And, worse still, encumbered with all kinds of dichotomy resulting from such bondage on every level: religious and cultural, social and existential. The cleavage of the sacred and the profane has indeed been ultimately the ransom for all the other cleavages that have marred Western thought: faith and reason, subject and object, God and man, being and nonbeing, lower and higher, inside and outside . . .

We've toppled God and eroded the sacred, we denounce objectification and are suspicious of subjectivism. But dualism we're not quite ready to let go of.

Instead, we fear technology, because it would affect the whole man. And we see it as we do Newspeak: a perversion of language.

What if just the opposite were the case? Could it be that through technology language has finally come into its own? Indeed, because technology does affect the whole man, we finally realize that what's needed is a new language, more consonant with a new type of religiosity emerging from the ruins of a sacral universe of discourse allowed by myth—a universe of discourse for which technique is reduced to magic, and speech to some wondrous speechlessness. A universe in which being, that which is, can only lie outside language, a mere tool, a rudimentary technique: utopia definitely lies less "nowhere"than outside this world.

Clearly, the basic dualism of the sacral universe of discourse has until now so affected our thinking and speaking that God-talk is still caught up in it. I will even claim that, under the regime of onto-theology, language was reduced to analogy, shorn as it was of its metaphoric power (like Newspeak or, better, like Lucky's speech in Beckett's *Waiting for Godot*). This would need arguing, surely. But I shall simply appropriate for myself a remark of Lacan's when he says that analogy is no metaphor,[6] and adds: analogy rests on Being, on the sacred (or vice versa), whereas metaphor is geared to the primacy of the word. Analogy turns language into a tool, at best into some annex of the human if not into an instrument of annexation. By contrast, metaphor fails if it does not underscore, indeed score, the verbal condition of reality, whether human or divine.

Just as in Christ there is neither Greek nor Jew, neither male nor female, so also is there in language neither God nor man.[7] Metaphor is iconoclastic, or it is not a metaphor.

Utopia versus the Sacred: From Mask (Persona) to Screen (Word)

Concomitant with the rise of technology, the emergence of linguistics and its cognates underlies a radical mutation of our sense for religion, whereby the latter, centered on logos is now beckoned no longer by the sacred but by utopia. Nor is this suprising. If demythologization is a necessity of the word (and especially therefore with faith), so is desacralization. What is needed now is to get rid of dualism, particularly if theology is to be liberated both from the analogy of being and the dialectic of the sacred and the profane.

Even linguistics appears to this day not to be immune from this dualism, though it should or could be. But vestiges are even harder to get rid of than is the real thing. And in our case, although language is nowadays seldom referred to some supernatural reality, the distinction between signifier and signified is still carried on in a way that inevitably betrays dualistic overtones, even if the signified is reduced to the signifier or is brought under the signifier over or across the bar that separates them. Indeed, I am concerned with that famous bar itself. What does it stand for? And am I entirely off the mark in claiming that it harks back to the age-old cleavage of sacred and profane and its variants from letter and spirit to reason and revelation? Not to mention the latest cleavage in vogue at least in some circles: the unconscious and—at the cost of a blasphemy—the other of the other?

Trying to investigate what the bar stands for, one could perhaps also invoke ethnology and the history of religions, and suggest it plays the same role as the mask. A mask meant to conceal a god less than the man who in fact wears it during ritual ceremonies of initiation. As if man himself were meant to hide himself from himself since he is transgressing the hierarchical order of things by being initiated into a higher world, into the world of the unsaid if not unsayable. But if one bears in mind that the unsaid is not necessarily commensurate with the *new*, the *novum* (*inédit* or *inouï*), it could perhaps be more readily accepted why the bar between signifier and signified can play the role of a mask. Like the dialectic of presence and absence, the dialectic of said and unsaid harks back to that of identity and difference: it fails, however, in attempting really to come to grips with the *other* with the otherness of the Other except at best in terms of opposition, like the opposition between God and man, being and nothingness, the sacred and the profane. Things are, so to speak, different enough to be complementary of one another, and eventually to the point of rivaling one another without mercy. But there is no idea of things as being compatible one with the other whether they are complementary of one another or not, or determined so to be beforehand.

Likening the bar to the mask may not be quite evident but is not so farfetched as it may sound, and evidence would not be hard to come by, given the structure of our Western mentality and the general conceptuality of our traditional worldviews. It would bear out the contention that the language of the mask is derived from presuppositions tying it to a mythological universe of discourse which is anchored in the sacred. Likewise a good deal of language analysis, even of hermeneutics, betrays to this day a mental atavism dangerously alienated by the erroneous if traditional assumption of salvation as the kernel of religion, as its exclusive kernel.

The evidence, however, would easily point out and confront the contention that, at least in the Western tradition, Greek as well as Judeo-Christian, religion is pegged on utopia: there is no world but this one in which man can live by faith and which he can and must therefore change. Even magic implies such a perspective! And today grammatology, by contrast with hermenuetics, is definitely motivated by this kind of orientation. From transgression to subversion the distance is the same as that between analogy and metaphor, the myth of man and the human as technique, changing worlds and changing the world, the sacred and utopia. Or between the mask and the screen. And the screen I see as the symbol of a mythological civilization. Indeed, ours is already the civilization of the screen.

Let's go back to the point that even the bar can be viewed as a screen. By contrast with the mask, for which there is an inside and an outside, a higher and a lower, a subject and an object, the screen does not stand between but behind and before both terms of each couple; it encompasses them. The mask is never dropped. If one term does not wear it the other does. Or else one could not be referred to the other, and vice versa. And there could be no *persona* either. And, likewise, no revelation. Should thus, for instance, the real stand revealed, it could only be from the standpoint of a *persona*, one who is subjected to the real if not, simply, subject to anything and everything that would seem more real than the real. By contrast, the screen works only to the extent that it disappears, and lets be. It alters itself if the *Other* must be, and be without having its otherness swallowed up in some dialectic of identity and difference. It does not hide this otherness, nor does it homogenize that which is heterogeneous as does the mask when it reveals by concealing and conceals by revealing. The screen deals with otherness, not with presence and absence as does the mask that hides or, for that matter, unveils. This is nothing else than *déjà vu,* albeit anamnestically.

Moreover, by contrast with the mask that must be seen, the screen must not. It follows, as strange as it may sound, that the mark of technological civilization lies less with image than with sound, less with analogy than with metaphor, the screen points *out,* it means: it tips image into word even if we have grown accustomed to designate by writing what previously was called text or if we tend to recognize traditions by reason of their *cultural* rather than *religious* heritage. Heritage in relation to which we act or continue to act as *voyeurs* rather than as *seers.* No wonder! A good deal of text criticism is today more akin to voyeurism than to prophecy. No longer is text a *screen.* Nor does it, like litmus paper (what the French call révélateur), reveal yet without hiding anything, whether the author's mind or some unsaid. Instead, it becomes a cliché: is the New Testament a cliché of the Old? Or, in another realm, is nature a cliché of grace? Screening entails no abrogating whether of nature by grace or of God by man.

And could that be the reason why scripture, indeed all scripture, is inspired of God? A God whose radical otherness stands or falls with the no less radical wholeness of man, compatible as they are without being complementary (much less rivals of one another), *encompassed* as they are by one and the same language—of the Word become flesh, of nature turned into creation, of history into destiny, of time into the fulness of time. And of the world into a new world.

I say: where myth was, there should be torah (or logos). Instead of *physis,* the Law (or *nomos*). Instead of *archē,* prolepsis. Instead of mother earth, the promised land. Instead of Babel, Pentecost.

Still, I say: no language cancels another without canceling itself. No scripture abrogates another without abrogating itself. Else it is not inspired by God. Scripture is without precedent just as writing is a *screen*—a trace, of which the origin disappears, through which the origin disappears. Revelation occurs neither at the beginning nor at the end of scripture. A poem does not come before or after language, but in spite of it as well as through it. Where a poem occurs, there is a new thing: language is surpassed by language. Like reason, then, revelation stands or falls with language. And the relation between the signifier and the signified would amount to a game of hide and seek should language be reducible to something either natural or supernatural.

Language and the Christ

In the Old Testament, God is a requirement of torah, not of nature, just as, in the New Testament, he is a requirement of the Christ event, not of history. He is an iconoclastic word about man, just as man is an iconoclastic word about God. Indeed, it has often been pointed out that in Genesis, by contrast with other such stories, man is understood preeminently, if not exclusively, in terms of his relation to God. A God who alone is God. Who is less the One than he is one, and much less an absolute or the craving for an absolute than he is that of which both the absolute and the quest of it fall short—the Other.

Not a stopgap either, as Paul points out when he says that the world is full of gods. In his view, the main thing lies in knowing that in Christ— and only in Christ—nothing can separate us from God if only because only through Christ is God so radically other that man need *not* sink in him, nor be shorn of his humanity as though he were castrated, and thus be alienated from him. Linguists talk of the primacy of the signifier over the signified. Could it be that Paul has already discovered this, yet without understanding it as implying any occultation of the Other by the other in terms of which the self comes into its own? Or, for that matter, as implying that the signified is necessarily eclipsed even while the signifier comes into his own. For in Christ it is not God that dies, but that which masks his otherness, whether on the grounds of some pantheistic naturalism or otherworldly monotheism. Or, as Paul puts it, no longer do we know Christ according to the flesh. We can only find him in Scripture.

But, then, does the same not apply to man? In and through Christ his is a verbal condition which is the very condition of God. And by the same token come to an end all types of dualism, from that of the signifier and the signified back to that of the sacred and the profane, the matrix of them all.

Like analogy, the sacred grows out of nature and returns to nature. To the *arche*. In the Old Testament, faith is not bound to nature or to any analogy of it but to its metaphor, to torah: religion is not confused with the sacred but is borne by utopian vision both of the human reality and the reality of the world. (Indeed, the lamb still is mostly viewed sacrificially when in fact, according to another trend, it could and should be viewed eschatologically: e.g., the lion and the lamb lying down together.)

Not *physis* but *techne* and its utopianism is what provides religion with a language, an instrument through which man puts up in the world and not merely with it. (The term 'pagan' is not so accidental as all that, either.) To be sure, the sacral universe was not entirely devoid of utopianism. Only, it groped after an unrealizable kind of utopia, thus overcompensating for the scarcity by which man is beset in this world. Today, we have to cope with the reverse problem, which has to do not so much with utopia's being realizable as with the need to choose between utopia and the "final solution." Indeed, they do not mix.

The latter too is realizable. But here as elsewhere realizable need not mean inevitable. Much less, therefore, does a realizable utopia need to imply the alienation of man. I would even argue that utopia is realizable only so long as man remains inalienable. Responsible. Which amounts to saying: outside language there is no utopia. As Lacan writes: "C'est le monde des mots qui crée le monde des choses, d'abord confondues dans l'hic et nunc du tout en devenir, en donnant son être concret à leur essence, et sa place partout à ce qui est de toujours: κτημα 'ξζ'αξι.

"L'homme parle donc, mais c'est parce que le symbole l'a fait homme."[8] He speaks. Nor does he speak because he has a mouth, but has a mouth because he speaks. He speaks, and a symbol turns him into a man. A symbol: that is not what links him to nature or, for that matter, to history; but what frees him from either. A symbol: that is, the structuring principle of language and its texture; a text, when the real and the ideal converge as do the natural and the artificial (*technē*), the body and the soul, and as do also the signifier and the signfied, the letter and the spirit. All scripture is inspired of God (Paul would say). Or, prodded by a former student to quote Henri Bosco: "All the being of the world, if it dreams, dreams that it is speaking." A symbol.

And therefore a text. To which one goes as one goes to the empty tomb on Easter morning: across the frontier of divine and human; that is, into language—the dawning of truth as emancipation as well as authentication of man. Only thus "wo Es war, soll Ich werden."[9] A new man, without precedent. And who, if it is true that God gave his only Son only because he so loved the world, speaks and thus entrusts the world with God.

Notes

1. Giorgio Agamben, "Propos . . ., "*Bulletin de l'Association freudienne*2 (1983):27.

2. "Verbum sine verbo, "*Le Discours psychanalytique* 6 (1983):65.

3. Jacques Lacan, "Postface," *Le Seminaire* II (Paris: Editions du Seuil, 1973), 253. Moustapha Safouan, *L'Inconscient et son scribe* (Paris: Editions du Seuil, 1982), 59.

4. Noam Chomsky, "Le langage est le miroir de l'esprit." *L'Anneé littéraire 1972*, La Quinzaine littéraire (Paris, 1973), 263.

5. Hans-George Gadamer, "Man and Language," *Philosophical Hermeneutics.* ed. and tr. David E. Linge (Berkeley: Univ. of California Press, 1976), 59-68 (see esp. 62-63).

6. "Fonction et champ de la parole et du langage (Discours de Rome)." *Ecrits* (Paris: Editions du Seuil, 1966), 262. (=Anthony Wilden & Jacques Lacan, *The Language of the Self* [Baltimore: Johns Hopkins Univ. Press, 1968], 24-25.) Cf. also "L'Instance de la lettre dans l'inconscient, où la raison depuis Freud," *Ecrits*, 508: ". . . la métaphore se place au point précis où le sens se produit dans le non-sens."

7. "Fonction et champ," 299: "Je m'identifie dans le langage, mais seulement à m'y perdre."

8. *Ecrits*, 276.

9. Lacan, "L'Instance," *Ecrits* 524, adds: "Quel est donc cet autre à qui je suis plus attaché qu'à moi, puisqu'au sein le plus assenti de mon identité à moi même, c'est lui qui m'agite?"

Summary

David Crownfield

Gabriel Vahanian's essay is not about Lacan's bearing on theological discourse. Vahanian is not a Lacanian. His essay is included in this collection because it deals with the theological question of the nature of language, and does so in a way that raises or intersects with many of the issues in Lacan. It is written in the context of an extensive awareness of what Lacan has said, and considerable thought and discussion about how that bears on theological matters, but it cites Lacan only twice, and in general resolutely refuses to permit him to establish the agenda of the discussion. I propose in this response to draw out what seem to me to be key themes in Vahanian's dense text and to juxtapose them with overtly Lacanian ideas and questions.

Language is utopian for Vahanian. This means not that it promises a reified actualization of our fantasies, but that it is the bearer of the unlimited openness and possibility of the human future. The structure of language is such that it is capable of saying anything: it always holds out the promise of the different, the possible, the unprecedented. (Neurotic and ideological distortions of language do not undermine this view because they only conceal but do not remove this radical promise, and it is indeed the capacity of the language to bear this utopian promise that is the locus of the possibility of overcoming neurosis and ideology.)

To speak is to have faith: to engage with the possibility of change and of changing the world. Meaning is the signifying accomplished in speech, which occurs as a projection of possible change of self and world. At the same time this speech is already located, in a sense signified, by the already-given texture of signification into which it occurs. In this futuring, signification is iconoclastic. Refiguring the world, it subverts the signified by the signifier, even as it speaks the subversion of the signifier by the signified.

Words in their differences, their contrasts, their oppositions insti-
gate pretenses, rivalries, strayings. What is lost and concealed in these
distortions is speechless, frustrating. Faith and reason, body and soul,
God and the human, are oppositions that conceal their inseparability
so long as they are not permitted to call each other into question.

To signify is to be anchored, marked, written out. The word God
occurs in the text of the "Word of God," but God is not the signified of
this signifier, but is other to both. Vahanian calls God *l'autre de l'autre*,
the other of the other; he is not so much disagreeing with Lacan's statement that there is no Other of the Other as affirming that God is
Other, not petit other.

Language is a technique. Not that language is a mere tool, external
to the subject and goal; technique is metaphor here, where technique
does not dehumanize but humanize, does not work by standardization
and rationalization but through treasuring its history, resisting its rationalization. The rationalization of technology and society itself requires
language, and can be achieved humanly only insofar as language itself
avoids its own rationalization. If it does not, we have the dystopic world
of *1984* and its allies, where language must be mutilated to maintain
the rationalization of society. A polarity of Newspeak and glossolalia is
the alternative to the unlimited utopianism of language.

A central issue for Vahanian is the contrast between the utopian
and the sacred. In his terminology, the sacred, nature religion analogy,
and metaphysics are put on the side of a notion of language that signifies
an extralinguistic other, like what Raschke calls magical language. Over
against these he puts the human, the utopian, metaphor, and technique. For the former, language functions as a sort of mask or visible
persona which *represents* the real, the divine, the significant that are
hidden behind it. For the latter, he uses the metaphor of a screen on
which, by means of which, otherness is displayed, allowed to appear.
The screen itself disappears, is merely the locus of the appearance of
what appears in its otherness. (In contrast, Taylor and Winquist, and
most deconstructive and Lacanian thought, consider it the task of contemporary writing to make the language-screen visible, acknowledging otherness precisely by making transparent the failure to present it.)

The very bar of separation/connection of signifier and signified
(S/s) is for Vahanian a mark of the dualism of the sacred, metaphysical, magical view. Signifiers are in the visible world; signifieds are some-
where else (for Saussure, in the mind; for realists, in a tranlinguistic
world; for psychoanalysis, in the unconscious. The bar itself serves as
mask, to present and simulate what is hidden behind it. For a Vahanian,
semiotics, in contrast, signifiers, are a screen, *on which* the world
appears in its reality and otherness. This is essentially equivalent to

Heidegger's understanding of language as the place where what-is occurs, is present-ed.

The discourse of the mask is myth (magical). The discourse of the screen is Torah, logos (signification under the Law of the Father). Revelation occurs in this language, on this screen (not behind it or anterior to it, or as a caused result of it). Revelation speaks of God as an iconoclastic way of speaking about the human; it speaks of the human as an iconoclastic way of speaking about God. It is language that makes the human human—even in the sense in which this has not yet been accomplished!

For Vahanian—as for Lacan, but differently—there is a split, a dislocation in the human subject, which is what it is not, and is not what it is. More than a Lacanian ex-centricity or a Sartrean formula of self-transcendence, this paradox is for Vahanian a matter of *simul justus ac peccator*. Human existence is faith, is the possibility of change and of changing the world, the generation of signifying acts which make meaning in the meaningless, transcending the bonds of both nature and history. Truth for the human is not in propositions, but in emancipation and authentication, which come in the utopianism of language, in the revelation of the word of God.

Vahanian does not disagree here with Lacan's notion of the ex-centric character of the subject, but he does not locate the problem in the essential nature of our linguistic being. There is for Vahanian, as there is not for Lacan, a possibility of authentic, whole subjectivity, a way to full human being that does not require castration. Language, in its full speech as word of God, brings this possibility as our name and our future. Freud's famous dictum, "Wo es war. Soll Ich werden [Where it was, I must come to be]," means for both Vahanian and Lacan that I must become subject of that from which I am alienated in repression and self-division; but for Vahanian this is the promise of the utopianism of language, the possibility of a true subject before the otherness of God.

God! Theological discourse, breaking out within these very pages! Is it possible? In order for God to be, there must be language. God is *verbum*. Not contained in language, which is no container, but being in language, rather than in being. A word, in the text, in the Word of God. God is the other of the other, the Other to the signified as well as to the signifier, in a sense like that developed in Wyschogrod's discussion of Anselm. God here is radically other, but is not the opposite or negative of the human or the world: rather, the abolition of such dualistic oppositions. God as the iconoclastic word about the human is the subversion of the pretense of the human to be identical with itself, adequate to itself, present subject of its own story. The human is at the same time an iconoclastic word about God, unmasking and deconstructing and demystifying. I would say, the human is the flesh in which are inscribed our words about God, and God's words about us. (But I am not sure Vahanian would put it that way.)

This is, indeed, a specifically Christian theology. Christ, as signifier of God, does not occult, is not barred from being transparent to, the signified. This signified, this God, is radically Other, so radically Other that it does not require our castration. Submitting to the Law of the Father as it is revealed by the self-giving Son, we are not mutilated but made whole. We do not have this wholeness as ego, but as promise and vocation. The absent subject, the Other, is the One who is promised and who promises. *In the language!* The being of God is not as Being, but is the life of this promise in this language, as the subject of the text of the Word of God.

This, as far as I can see it, is Vahanian's position, read in the light of these essays on Lacan (and also of several long conversations with Vahanian about this essay, recollected after my own engagement with the texts of Lacan). There are several evident points at which it might be questioned. Is a purely linguistic being of God capable of bearing a utopic promise, of making possible an entry into language, the Law of the Father, that does not castrate but transforms and heals? Is the absence in Vahanian of consideration of the role of desire in language, and of the illusory character of desire, tenable? (Perhaps on the ground that the radical otherness of the promise is the fulfilment rather than the vacating of desire?) Is the negation of the natural, the relegation of the body to silence, in fact utopian or escapist?

A critical question here seems to me to be about the Real. For Lacan, the Real is what limits, what is impossible, what imposes itself on the signifying structures. The Real irrupts in birth, in need, in pain, in orgasmic *jouissance*, in death. It is the body that bears the brunt of the real; and for Vahanian the body is silent. Language is truly utopian for Vahanian, bearer of all goods and healer of all ills. While for Lacan it is in bringing desire to speech that the suffering of the neurotic is eased, for Vahanian, the very pain of the Real can be overcome in language. I have difficulty with this not only from a psychoanalytic standpoint: theologically, it seems ultimately to be a docetism, a doctrine of the Christ who dies only in the text.

Perhaps not. This is a difficult essay, and Vahanian is a rich and subtle thinker. I may, in quest of a conclusion, misread him. The only cure for that is to read him again, which is well worth doing.

7.

Religion and Television

William James Earle

"Television," in the title, is meant to signify in two ways. *First*, it refers to Lacan's *Télévision*, where the connection between surprise and the unconscious is pithily expressed. *Second*, it refers to actual television, a realm of distinction without difference where the real world is recycled wearing the colors of specious glamour.

The first section of this paper explains how psychoanalysis refutes certain crucial assumptions shared by thinkers from the Enlightenment through classical utilitarianism. Given those assumptions (and the expectations they standardly generate) it is surprising religion did not disappear wherever Western culture held sway. Psychoanalysis helps explain this resilience. But there are two diametrically opposite interpretations of, or morals to be drawn from, the nondisappearance of religion: (1) The Enlightenment has to be pushed forward — personally and publicly — with the new resources made available by psychoanalysis. This is, very clearly, the view of Freud. (2) We ought to give up on the Enlightenment, which is now seen to be a fundamentally defective vision of human life, human possibility. Whether or not Lacan thought this, it is the view of some who style themselves Lacanians. At the end of section one, I try to say why Freud is right. The Enlightenment seriously underestimated cognitive waywardness, but to abandon the Enlightenment for that reason would be like abandoning probability theory because people persist in making bad bets.

The second section of this essay focuses on one of the crucial Enlightenment assumptions, the assumption that desires can be — fairly straightforwardly — satisfied, that unsatisfied desires are unsatisfied contingently or accidentally, and that there is no intrinsic limitation to progress toward complete satisfaction of human desire. This is the assumption [to put it in convenient shorthand] that desires are, characteristically, *needlike*. Needlikeness does not indicate a constraint on the *content* of desires; it picks out a *form* of desire, just the form that psychoanalysis says desires, paradigmatically and *par excellence*, fail to have. Put positively, psychoanalysis says desires "televise" their objects. "Televise" is, of course, metaphorical: a metaphor for allure-generating distantiation. Unpacking this metaphor, and saying why it catches something important, are main tasks of section two.

The third section of this essay explores the connection between the psychoanalytic concept of desire and religion. As conceived by psychoanalysis, desires idolize their objects. To this pervasive idolatry René Girard refers in the title of the second chapter of *Mensonge romantique et vérité romanesque:* "Les hommes seront des dieux les uns pour les autres."[1] Why are we gods for each other? Why does passion worship its objects from a distance impossible to cross? Why does sexual, or "romantic," love generate a kind of superstitious cult of the beloved? It must make a difference, in answering these questions, whether one believes in God or not. Those who do, have a real concept of idolatry, the name of a kind of sin; the rest have an interesting metaphor. And there should be other differences—at least if it matters, in explaining why people believe that p, whether we ourselves think that p is true. But even to raise this issue is to suppose a cognitive orientation that can identify and assess the truth claims of religious beliefs and of beliefs about the objects of our desires. This orientation has been challenged; so Mary Douglas, reviewing Peter Brown's *The Making of Late Antiquity,* writes: "If anthropology has anything to say to history, it is to suggest that the spiritual beings in which people believe are not interesting to the believers in an academic or theoretical sense. They are interesting at a particular time because they can credibly intervene in particular ways."[2] But there is still a theoretical sense to worry about and the blunt question of how credible intervention relates to existence. This is, I suppose, an Enlightenment question, the question of people who think there can be a conflict between religion and science, people who are attached to such concepts as "evidence" and "reasonable belief." What do such concepts become for someone who assigns the unconscious its full theoretical, and indeed theory-disestablishing, significance? This is Lacan's theme of "la raison depuis Freud."[3] What is at issue, we should underline, is the conception of "reason," not its replacement with "antireason," and the correlative understanding of such terms as 'science,' 'theory,' 'evidence,' and 'reasonable belief.' Is there reason to think that, despite Freud's own hostility, "la raison depuis Freud" is more friendly to religion than reason was before? This is a large question which, even phrased in general and perhaps recklessly undifferentiated terms ("religion," "reason"), can be looked at in a number of ways. Some of these (by way of illustration rather than inventory) will figure in section three.

The fourth (and final) section of this paper might be titled "la raison depuis Lacan." What is new about "la raison depuis Lacan"? For Lacan himself, the fundamental discovery was Freud's; he named *his* school [Ecole Freudienne de Paris, founded in 1964] and the series of associated books [Seuil, le champ freudien, collection dirigée par Jacques Lacan] after Freud, and much of his work was detailed — albeit *sui generis* — commentaries on, or reflections inspired by, texts of Freud. As Malcolm Bowie put it: "Lacan reads Freud. This is the simplest and most important thing about him."[4] But it would be wrong to see Lacan as disciple, exegete, interpreter. For one thing, he is suspicious of what he sees as Freud's *scientificity* where 'scientificity'refers to science as a limited, time-bound enterprise, to science's about-to-be shed late-nineteenth-century carapace. By temperament and commitment, Lacan is a kind of polymathic poet, methodological pluralist, artist of allusion, ambivalence, and disequilibration. In the "ouverture du séminaire" he writes (and the allusion to Plato is characteristic):

> It works in psychoanalysis as in the art of the good cook who knows how to carve up an animal, to detach the articulated parts with the least resistance. One knows that there is, for each structure, a mode of conceptualization proper to it. But as that leads to complications [on entre par là dans la voie de complications], one prefers to stick to the monistic notion of a deduction of the world. So one goes astray.[5]

The *voie de complications* may be onerous and *prima facie* rebarbative, but it is not meant to be inherently confusing, and it is, in any case, the only way the analyst can recover "le registre du sens" or the "subjectivity of the subject, in his desires, in his relation to his milieu, to other people, to life itself."[6]

Rather than attempt summary or interpretive synthesis (which would miscarry in the case of Lacan for much the same reason it miscarries in the case of Wittgenstein), section four considers a single, though central, topic: the "linguistic turn" Lacan imparts to psychoanalysis. Whether or not we ought to speak of a "structuralist psychoanalysis" in this connection, Lacan certainly relied on the work of Saussure, the single ancestral common denominator of all French structuralisms. I hasten to add that "relied on" does not mean "built on" — at least as understood according to the model, or myth, of progressive/cumulative scientific linearity. About Lacan *vis-à-vis* Saussure, Jean-Luc Nancy and Philippe Lacoue-Labarthe write: "None of the concepts of the theory of the sign disappears: signifier, signified, signification are still there. But there system is twisted, perverted."[7] Section four tries to say what Saussure's "theory of the sign" amounts to and what Lacan does with it.

Enlightenment Assumptions

Allow me to begin this section with an incidental illustration. Everytime I see people playing three-card monte (a version of the ancient shell game commonly played on the sidewalks of New York) I am astonished anew, not that there are people willing to con, but that there are people left to be conned. Three-card monte is a very well-known, well-advertised, scam, and additionally, it wears its illegitimacy rather blatantly. One thinks: if it is seen at all, it can be seen through. Like everything "one thinks," this thought has a history, is not spontaneously generated. It is in fact, in the rough-and-ready way I am using the term, an Enlightenment thought, the thought that there is such a thing as *neutral observation* that catches the *naturally salient* features of what is observed. We get the benefit of neutral observation by stripping away presuppositions (often derived from a bookish or "scholastic" tradition) and other kinds of interferences, distortions, idols. It is now generally recognized that Bacon's purified empiricist program involves an idea — that of preconceptionless observation — that is very nearly empty and that Bacon pinned his exorbitant hopes on an intellectual fiction. One way of saying what Bacon missed is to say that observation is driven by theory, that theory produces salience, determines relevance and importance. Another way of saying the same thing, closer to the concerns of this paper, is to say that observation is necessarily conditioned by language. So this turns out to be an instance of Lacan's "omniprésence du discours humaine."[8]

A dog, despite sharp eyes and olfactory acuity, doesn't see three-card monte: probably no concept of game, certainly no concept of fraudulent game. Of course the people on the street who are duped have these concepts, but they are still conceptually somewhat under-equipped. If they speak English what they need is the word *shill*, in any case, that concept: apparent winner in collusion (or cahoots) with the dealer. I should add that it is possible on the spot to invent the concept shill based on observed regularities, or prevalent patterns, in the dealer's payouts: the money always goes to the same person. But; whether inherited or invented, *shill* (or something like the phrase it abbreviates) has to be put into play in the complete correct analysis of three-card monte. This leads to a penultimate remark. Objectivity, defined in terms of getting it right or not getting it right, does not depend on, and so does not disappear with, observational neutrality. Finally, is there an implied comparison with religion? Is religion really supposed to be like three-card monte? (If I were a religious person and somebody suggested this, I would stop reading his paper.) Fortunately, the answer is a qualified no rather than a qualified yes. The analogue of collusion in the case of religion is conspiracy and conspiracy theories of religion, though occasionally advanced, are not very promising. Further, a whole game of three-card monte takes place in a chunk of the specious present, or more-or-less *hic et nunc*, which means (first) that it should be possible to acquire evidence about payouts that are not supposed — by anybody — to be deferred and (second) that therefore there doesn't seem to be room for the operation of faith. In the case of — at least — classical Christianity, there is a barrier to the acquisition of evidence about payouts because, they are deferred to the hereafter and so there is plenty of room for faith, that is, belief unsupported by evidence.

I should say, by way of clarification, that I don't want to equate religion with belief in otherworldly payouts or rewards *à la* Marc Connelly's *Green Pastures*. Religion may also (and perhaps better) be thought of as the worship of God *now*, because of its deep intrinsic cognitive/affective appropriateness, with no thought of *tomorrow*. But I take it that, on this view too, there is room for faith.

Faith is hard to write about because faith generates an inside and an outside between which there is incommensurability, irreconcilable difference. From the point of view of faith, having faith is a good thing. From the outside, faith may seem like a reaction formation to evidence, rationally defensible belief, established knowledge. And from the outside, the nondisappearance of religion may seem like, or somewhat like, the street robustness of three-card monte. The Enlightenment saw credulity as exhaustible and nonselfrenewing so the continued playability of three-card monte occasions surprise. We may wonder from what position, what *Lebensform* location, the question "Is faith a type of credulity?" 'may be asked both fairly and usefully.

The Enlightenment assumption so far discussed, that is, the assumption that there is such a thing as neutral observation, did not require anything peculiar to psychoanalysis to defeat it. One can view the correction of Bacon's naive empiricism by later, and better, philosophers of science as a correction which left the basic Enlightenment picture unaltered. There is, however, a seemingly anodyne, hardly noticeable component of that assumption, the idea of "the observer," which has begun to disintegrate only in this century, with psychoanalysis a major, though not the only, agent of disintegration, disestablishment. My astonishment when I see three-card monte derives from my seeing each player as an observer, thought of as a Cartesian ego, *res cogitans*, or mind: a punctual, highly self-transparent, self-knowing, absolutely unclouded, unoccluded, inertia-free consciousness. I then locate plausible three-card monte-player thoughts within this unified system of all-or-nothing, or gradient-free, awareness. This is, however, to substi-

tute a schematic philosophical construction for the actual inner lives of
the players, players who half-know they're going to lose but half-believe
they're going to win, who are dimly aware of anomalies, have feelings
they suppress rather than act on, and are [to put it generally] a whole
lot more complicated, and denser, than Cartesian egos.

The street phenomena are not marginal, not beneath theoretical
notice, certainly not the occasion for smug self-distantiation. Freud has
taught us this: a subject or "eigene Person" (Freud's term for person as
individual)[9] is much more complicated, much less available for summary identification, than in the main post-Cartesian tradition. Althusser,
in an essay titled "Freud et Lacan," provides a statement of Freud's
contribution to philosophy which emphasizes just this point: "Freud
showed us ... that the real subject, the individual in his singular
essence, does not have the form [figure] of an ego, centered on the 'I'
[moi], on consciousness, or on existence—whether this is the existence
of the "for-itself" [pour-soi], of one's own body, or of behavior [comporte-
ment],—that the human subject is decentered, constituted by a structure itself without center, except in the imaginary misrecognition of
the 'I,' that is to say, in ideological formations where the 'I' recognizes
itself."[10] One of those ideological formations is the law (the standard
legal system) which assigns responsibility, by way of a defensible and
useful fiction, to a singular agent, the punctual producer of ex nihilo
volitions, whereas the real "eigene Person," as Benvenuto and Kennedy
put it, "seems to have a psychical apparatus made up of various agen-
cies, each of which has distinct properties and functions, and which
interact dynamically and in conflict with each other."[11] Philosophers
may regard this dispersal of agency as renascent homunculism and in
fact many analysts practiced—indeed continue to practice—their trade
as a kind of reductive ego-hardening. Lacan polemicized against both
the philosopher's dismissal of Freud's discoveries as a congeries of category mistakes and his own confreres' revisionist "normalization" of psychoanalysis into a form of ego psychology.

Probably most philosophical treatments of belief still amount to
ego psychology. I mention this conceptual area because it is relevant to
our understanding of the people playing three-card monte. We ascribe
beliefs to the players of three-card monte as anthropologists ascribe
beliefs to their natives. We may be, and the anthropologists may be,
very scrupulous in characterizing the contents of beliefs, but what may
not be faced is "la pluralité des modalités de croyance." This phrase is
from the introduction Paul Veyne's Les Grecs ont-ils cru à leurs mythes?[12]
Veyne's point is that no simple answer can be given to the title's
question: his book is an exercise in analytical/historical complication.
One of the modalities of belief, operative in minor irrationalities and

in the petty superstitious practices of everyday life, O. Mannoni evokes with the phrase (which titles an essay dealing with the phenomenon) "Je sais bien; mais quand même . . ." [I know very well, but all the same . . .][13] I know very well the horoscopic prediction means nothing, but all the same I read it with a peculiar fascination. I know very well that walking under this ladder won't bring bad luck really, but all the same I don't walk under it. I know very well this woman isn't my mother, but all the same I avoid sleeping with her. A final illustration is provided by Serge Leclaire, a practicing member of Lacan's school. Leclaire tells us that all the sophisticated Parisians who enter analysis know they have Oedipus complexes, but that this knowledge has in general zero therapeutic value.[14] What is the difference between the doxastic component of zero-value knowledge and that of knowledge that cures and heals and redeems? This is not answered, nor even asked, by ordinary accounts of knowledge or belief.

Complication is sometimes used to support an antitheoretical or antiobjectivist stance (this seems to involve the *nonsequitur* that if things are complicated, they must be impenetrably complicated), but the complication evoked in the preceding paragraphs is itself generated by the search for adequate theory and the collapse of previous theory. The more complicated picture of the psyche offered by Freud and subscribed to by Lacan is an improvement on Enlightenment psychology because it is objectively more correct. If you have ever thought of yourself as a Cartesian ego immediately and remainderlessly available to itself, you may find the newer picture messy, but you should accept it because that's the way the psyche is. To speak of the objectively correct or more correct or of the way things are does betray a commitment to truth, but not to metaphysical realism or truth-as-correspondence. Truth (to schematize a very complicated matter) gets its point from the idea of getting something right or more right than one has, or someone else has, before, that is, from the idea of cognitive advance. Lacan's Freud and Lacan himself are part of this cognitive advance: referring to *Das Unbehagen in der Kultur*, Lacan remarks with obvious approval that Freud never abandons reason, never says *"Ici commence l'opaque et l'ineffable."*[15] I read this as affirming a central Enlightenment commitment.

What is not, cannot be, endorsed is Enlightenment psychology, or optimism about cognitive advance, or the view that impediments to enlightenment are all external. We know (when we are not forgetting it, not backsliding into complacency) that there is plenty of internal inertia, opacity, self-renewing, barely defeasible, obtuseness and that the psyche is a not altogether stable confederation of agents and double agents playing their own games, of actors at crosspurposes, of inconsistent voices, of mutually subversive energies.

The Hopelessness of Desire

The intellectual mastery of nature (which, contrary to Bacon's expectations, turned out to be a polymorphous and essentially interminable project) was supposed in the Enlightenment mainstream to entail a progressive reduction in scarcity and a correlative improvement in the material circumstances of humankind. Currents of progressivism, optimism, meliorism, and a commitment to reformism in politics—minimally, to the elimination of gross (that is, pre-Modern) privilege from the domain of political economy—came together in what was perhaps their last authoritative and fully confident statement in John Stuart Mill. After Mill, either our confidence that prosperity would trickle down to the least advantaged, or our confidence that any trickle could be enough, began to crumble. But we are not, here, interested in political or economic criticisms of Mill and the liberal tradition. Indeed criticism of the assumption that desires are "needlike" brings out something not ordinarily noticed by political or economic theory.

Politics, economics, political economy are all, from various angles, concerned with the provision—particularly, the distribution—of goods and services that satisfy desires that are needlike. (If linguistic stipulation had any chance of success, one might for the sake of clarity propose saving "desire" for the paradigmatically nonneedlike.) One can have a "political economy of hunger" because the desire for food is, paradigmatically, needlike. What does this mean? One should, for reasons I have discussed at length elsewhere.,[16] resist equating needlikeness with biological "necessity" or organism-indispensibility. As mentioned in the introductory section, the central, and criteriological, characteristic of needlike desires is that, if they are unsatisfied, they are contingently or accidentally unsatisfied. This is not to say that it is easy to satisfy needlike desires nor to deny that there are conceptual difficulties to be sorted out in our understanding of their insatisfaction. For example, one has to work out the relations between (in Sen's terms) "The Availability Approach" (How much food is there?) and "The Entitlement Approach" (Who has claims against the food supply? How are such claims generated?) bearing in mind that "starvation is a matter of some people not *having* enough food to eat, and not a matter of there *being* not enough food to eat."[17] Still, barriers to satisfaction, whether supply-based or claims-based, are all external. The problems of starving people are not psychological, not based on fantasies of food that can't be matched by real food. The desire for food, individual or aggregate, is finite; and, despite the cultural variability of expectation and taste, the concept of satiety can be given definite content. (Food can, of course, be "eroticized" and eating disordered, made symbolic or compensatory;

and there is even a pornography of food [magazines like *Gourmet*] — consumed, it is true, by the well-fed.)

The paradigm of the nonneedlike is sexual desire, and indeed, in the psychoanalytic tradition, discourse about desire is discourse about sexual desire. There is, Lacan says, something "enigmatic" about desire from the point of view of "philosophie naturelle,"[18] and this remark can be extended to politics, economics, political economy. We may ask, with perplexity or exasperation, "What does desire want?" but our question embodies a misassimilation: desire is not a kind of wanting, has no specifiable object, no finite fulfillment. Finally, desire [in the psychoanalytic sense] does not allow anything like direct application of the type/token distinction. This too is meant to be definitional or at least criteriological. Let me try to say why this characterization of desire is not mere paradox-mongering. It is likely that demonstration of the plausibility and pertinency of the psychoanalytic conception of desire, and the correlative overcoming of commonsense resistance, can only be achieved through the appreciation of "cases" (histories of uncovering histories/"Méthode, de vérité et de démystification des camouflages subjectifs"),[19] including an appreciation of oneself as an ambulatory instance of more of the same; but some of the complexity, sacrificing instantiality, can be schematized under the following headings: "sexuality and biology," "sexuality and insatisfaction," "sexuality and hallucination."

Sexuality and Biology. Referring to *Drei Abhandlungen zur Sexualtheorie*, Lacan uses the phrase "recouverts pour la foule par tant de gloses pseudo-biologiques"[20] which might be translated "covered over for the crowd by a bunch of pseudobiological glosses." A principal virtue of Lacan is to have achieved a consistently nonbiological reading of Freud. I remark in passing that in the Standard Edition, which dominates the English and American market, James Strachey chose to translate Freud's *Trieb* by "*instinct*" despite the fact that, as Laplanche and Pontalis note, "In Freud, one finds the two terms used in contradistinction [dans des acceptations nettement distinctes]. When Freud talks of *Instinkt*, it is to qualify the behavior of an animal which is fixed by heredity, species specific, preformed in its sequentiation [déroulement], and adapted to its object."[21] These are not "merely terminological" matters — if, as Lacan leads us to doubt, "merely terminological" isn't a contradiction in terms. We grasp the nature of sexuality — "human sexuality" is a pleonasm since only humans have sexuality — by denying each clause in the definition of "instinct." *First*, sexuality is not fixed by heredity: to the highly variable extent that it settles down on a set of persons, practices, and fantasies, "fixation" is determined by individual history, just what psychoanalysis reconstructs. *Second*, sexuality is not uniform across the species; if it were, perversions would have the same statistical distribution in the human population as abnormal, or defective, dam-building amongst beavers or abnormal, or defective, nest-building among birds. In fact, as everyone seems to agree, there are large numbers of perverts. (We should not be seduced, Freud warns us, by the "Gleichförmigkeit der normalen Gestaltung."[23] Third, sexual behavior isn't "preformed." Instinctual behavior, triggered by a very small number of invariant stimuli, unrolls in the same way time after time in animal after animal. Instinctual behavior plays an unalterable prerecorded tape, plays out a predetermined destiny; whereas sexuality plays, improvises, invents. Fourth, sexuality has no object in the sense of telos, which is what Laplanche and Pontalis mean by 'object'. (In the article on "instinct," where they give a definition corresponding to that quoted above, they say instinct appears "répondre à une finalité.")[22] Of course humans have teloi, recognize some teloi—and some routes to some teloi—as morally acceptable, and can, with good reasons or not, stipulate a single telos (procreation, fun, scientific experimentation, whatever) for sexuality and recommend, or enforce, the stipulation as may be.

The idea dies hard that "sexuality" picks out an ahistorical, essentially biological, phenomenon. Michel Tournier, in his answer to the question what was so extraordinary about Denis de Rougemont's Love in the Western World, writes: "Human love is not solely the product of a biological fatality. It supposes, certainly, an anatomo-physiological infrastructure, but, on this base, society, or rather societies, construct a code, a mythology, an edifice of dreams and sentiments which depend only on cultural factors. So love—in the sentimental sense of the term—dates from the eleventh century . . . ."[24] Freud and Lacan, talking about sexuality and desire, must be understood as making culture-circle-relative generalizations. It would not be at all surprising (nor disconfirming of Freud/Lacan) to find a tribe with no sexuality, no nonneedlike desire, free of our disease. There would be nothing mysterious about such a tribe: its attitudes toward acts which for us are sexual would simply resemble the attitudes of the well-fed toward eating. The acts would be performed (with a range of enthusiasm), procreation would take place, the tribe would perdure.

Sexuality and Insatisfaction. To credit desire with a direct aim at its own insatisfaction would indeed involve an unacceptable contradiction; but this contradiction, if it is anywhere, is in the inaccurate rational reconstruction of how desire works. It would be more accurate to say that desire connives at its own insatisfaction, sliding by particular objects that are treated as if they were mere advertisements (or signs) of desirability itself. So sexuality is a kind of disease or restlessness; and sexual desires are vagrant, wandering, disloyal. (It makes sense to say to people by way of moral advice: *Don't be like your desires!*)

Lacan says desire is always "désir d'autre chose [desire is for something else],"[25] that "le désir de l'homme est une métonymie [human desire is a metonymy]."[26] Desire is counterpractical, counterprudential: for it, a bird in the hand is not worth two, but *less than one*, in the bush. There is at least some similarity between the psychoanalytic (Freudian/Lacanian) conception of desire and Elster's *"counter adaptive preference,"* which he associates with the saying "forbidden fruit is sweet" and regards as a "perverse mechanism of want formation"[27] that is seen in "the perverse drive for novelty and change."[28] Desire is inherently transgressive, subverting worthy attempts to construct stable structures paying out perhaps quite modest, but also relatively dependable, rewards. Marriage is, of course, the most important of such structures. How it works, and fails to work, is the theme of Tony Tanner's *Adultery in the Novel*, subtitled "Contract and Transgression."[29] Marriage sometimes works and sometimes doesn't: when it does work, it doesn't work by satisfying sexual desires, but by replacing that project, *en bloc*, with the project of satisfying needlike (and single-person-sized) desires which are, in fact, related to the same anatomophysiological infrastructure as sexual desires. Since sexuality manages, whatever *we* may be thinking, to make itself sound glamorous and alluring—manages to metonymize itself or tease us—I want to say explicitly that I am a friend of marriage and marriage-like institutions and, to that extent, an enemy of desire.

Sexuality and Hallucination. We begin with what Freud calls "die Überschätzung des Sexualobjektes [the overvaluation of sexual objects] and an associated "Gläubigkeit der Liebe [credulity of love]."[30] This is, in a way, the learned reprise of "Love is blind," though it might be more accurate to say that love isn't looking. The most important component of overvaluation, or "overestimation" (as *Uberschatzung* might also be translated), consists in assigning central causality to a mere catalyst. We don't like to think of the people who trigger our erotic interest as having such an incidental, occasional, and finally purely accidental, role; we want our arousal to be provoked by their real qualities. These qualities, moreover, are supposed to be, in some degree, rare; and this is true even if we are aroused by any member of some class. This is nicely exhibited in the following passage from Proust—quoted by Girard: "If by chance I perceive it doesn't matter which of the young girls, since they all participate in the same special essence, it's as if I have seen projected in front of me, in a mobile and diabolical hallucination, a little of an inimical, yet passionately coveted, dream. . . ."[31] Of course Marcel, on the promenade at Balbec, isn't the man on the Clapham omnibus; still there is something of general significance expressed in the Proustian extreme. First we have to appreciate how puzzling it really is that sexuality should fall under the law of scarcity, since its raw material, other people, is plentiful. How can other people, who are after all much like ourselves, be thought to possess a special essence, a distinctive metaphysical sparkle?

Part of the answer lies in the sheer otherness of the other. It may be that otherness is just an overdramatized version of numerical distinctness misconstrued as asymmetrical, but the overdramatization and the misconstrual are not Lacan's (who is here a faithful reporter) but the psyche's. We should add that "the psyche" does not refer to a kind of natural object bound by natural laws (in the natural science sense) to have the interests in and reactions to other people detailed by psychoanalysis. There is no reason to suppose the mythology, the dramaturgy, in whose grip we live out—what Lacan calls—"toute *l'opera-buffa* humaine,"[32] grips everybody in quite the same way.

One other feature of sexuality, of desire, that seems relevant here is its more-than-contingent connection with fantasy: a tribe without fantasies would have no sexuality, no sexual desires. It is worth asking why fantasy (possibly accompanied by masturbation) doesn't put all real sexual, erotic, amatory, romantic effort out of business. The reason seems to be that fantasy suffers crucially from—in George Ainslie's phrase—"a shortage of scarcity."[33] One might then suggest that fantasy can't fantasize a reality having the same crucial defect as itself: it has to fantasize a reality in which scarcity is relatively plentiful. The main ways it does this are through hallucination of invidious distinction and through the delusional equation, or fusion, of unattainability and sexual allure.

This leads, finally, to the sense in which desires may be said to televise their objects. I am assuming here, to make the metaphor work, that the difference between people on television and people not on television is that the people on television are on television: their difference from the rest of us is otherwise nil. Nevertheless the medium that presents them awards them—automatically and unselectively—an unearned, or specious, glamour. Girard: "La surface de la terre où habitent les *Autres* devient un inaccessible paradis [the surface of the earth where the *Others* live becomes an inaccessible paradise]."[34] TV creates a kind of inaccessibility (more precisely, an intimation of inaccessibility); so do movies; so do gossip columns; so did the stories Proust listened to about those who had—what he called—a "belle position mondaine."[35]

All that one has to assume, to complete the metaphor, is that desire works as a presentational medium, presenting its objects as if they came from another world. Of course one can interface with the objects of one's desires, but then one's desires (though not one's needs) will be someplace else. One does, at least if one lives in New York or Los Angeles, run into TV stars who, in person, cease to glow. Proust's narrator, finally invited *chez les Guermantes*, is disappointed because they and their guests are more-or-less like everybody else. Marcel attempts to save his hypothesis of difference; as Girard summarizes, "He almost convinces himself, during that first night, that his profane presence has interrupted the aristocratic mysteries whose celebration cannot be continued while he is there."[36] Three comments conclude this section. *First*, The Proust/Marcel example is directly relevant here because snobbery is, in fact, the eroticizing of social relations. Snobbery works well, as an example to think about, because most of us have no, or little, investment in, or commitment to, snobbery: so we can see it very clearly as a generator of invidiousness. *Second*, there is the question of whether we should fight against disenchantment like Marcel or cultivate it like a Stoic sage. It is possible to train the eye to see the skeleton beneath the delectable flesh, to see the viscera awash in fluids inside the voluptuous body, to see everybody's age, death, and physical corruption. Is this a worthwhile project? *Third*, it might be objected that the difference between A whom I desire and B whom I do not is not nil. Of course this is true: two humans are never — can't be — merely numerically distinct. Still Girard's formula captures something important: *"une différence nulle engendrant une affectation maximum."*[37] There is something special about les Guermantes, but it is, literally, nominal, purely significant.

Desire and Religion

What conclusion can be drawn about religion from the low comedy of desire? One answer is suggested by René Girard, whose book, from which we have been quoting throughout, has as its epigraph Max Scheler's "Man possesses either a God or an idol." Either we worship God or we idolize each other: so the moderns who have stopped worshipping God have begun to worship each other. Since humans are not adorable, the attempt generates "toute *l'opera-buffa* humaine," the low comedy of desire, and characteristically modern forms of disappointment and despair. I hasten to add that nothing quite so schematic, or as explicitly moral-drawing, is found in Girard. Still the question remains whether we ought to see in the phenomena exposed by psychoanalysis a hunger for the infinite, an appetite for the transcendental, a properly religious desire, operating in a failed state and *faute de mieux*. Then we should have to consider whether this hunger (if we found it) could possibly form the basis of some kind of ontological argument.

In the case of Lacan, either this last question does not come up or, as Edith Wyschogrod suggests (see pp. 97-114), it is answered negatively. In the passage where Lacan says desire is enigmatic and always desire for something else (which can be given a religious twist), Lacan uses, still about desire, the phrase

> sa frénésie mimant le gouffre de l'infini

translated "its [desire's] frenzy mimics the abyss of the infinite."[38] This is, in Lacan's mouth, beautiful poetry, but also exact. Frenzy, a kind of precipitate, opportunistic, and exasperated longing, can only generate the "bad infinite" of repetition. What it mimics or apes or mocks or mimes (and so may be argued to know) is something purely—and spectacularly—a negative: an abyss, a big hole. Furthermore, Lacan is not offering his view of desire-as-frenzy as a diagnosis of the modern condition. He is not a cultural critic telling us where we went wrong. He thinks humans have always been going wrong and probably always will be—with margins of historical difference, moments and pockets of relative enlightenment. Like Freud, he does not say very much about the spatio-temporal parameters of his generalizations, though he obviously understands himself to be dealing with something basic and pervasive.

I turn, finally, to the question (raised in the introductory section) of reason and religion since Freud. In the wake of a political revolution, every faction tries to turn the massive dislocations, the temporarily fluid or at least unclear conditions, the vacua of power, to its own advantage. The same thing happens after so-called "Copernican" revolutions. After Copernicus's Copernican revolution, one faction said: This shows that biblical geocentrism is false and so is any Bible-based religion. Another faction said: This shows that we live in just the kind of universe you would expect an infinite God to create. After Freud's Copernican revolution, one faction said: This shows what a childish, pathetic, retrograde deception religious belief amounts to. Another faction said: This shows how much deeper the human mind, and how much more mysterious the universe (that after all contains that mind) is than anything dreamed of by Descartes and the facile materialists he—inadvertently—inspired.

There is likely to be difficulty-verging-on-impossibility in finding a position from which to adjudicate these contests that has any chance of satisfying all the contestants. Put the problem another way: How can we, this far into the discussion, find anything that does not have the form of ever more insistent repetition, like the interminable rehashing of frozen positions in a family quarrel? Put the problem still another way: What would make the disagreement between religious and nonreligious people tractable if it isn't tractable already?

One last point that may, I am afraid, itself have the flavor of insistent repetition. Some people believe that the concept of reality has been fundamentally destabilized by the Freudian revolution and that it is no longer convincing to say that some things are real (like tables, chairs, dogs, frogs, viruses, and electrons) and some things are not (like Santa Claus, unicorns, witches, phlogiston, honest politicians, and hell). The older view would be that, although we might disagree about what to put on each list, make mistakes, and change our minds, we would not disagree about the point of having two lists. My own — completely common-sensical — view is that the idea of the two lists is more fundamental than any theory, scientific or metaphysical, about what reality amounts to and is secure against all varieties of epistemological worry. I regard challenges to the two-lists idea as more-or-less impertinent, more-or-less crazy. From this point of view, it is quite natural to see any theoretical revolution, including the Freudian, as just making — maybe wholesale — changes in the two lists' contents. Is it cheating for you to reply, "Fine, let's just put List A on List B among the other fictions"? I think it is, but the account of why it is belongs someplace else. Here I simply want to emphasize something I hope is true. To believe in the two lists idea (so I hope) does not make one a participant in, or partisan of, what Lacan describes as "la dégradation de la psychanalyse, consécutive à sa transplantation américaine."[39] (1966; p. 68) In its degraded American transplantation (though not exclusively there), as Lacan understands these matters, psychoanalysis becomes a process of "réadaptation du patient au réel"[40] wherein, what is even worse, "it's the ego of the analyst which provides the yardstick of the real [c'est l'ego de l'analyste qui donne mésure du réel]."[41] In Lacan's idiolect, "the real" becomes, accordingly, the name for what is imposed on the patient and contrasted with what Lacan always refers to as the patient's own truth — truth of desire, subjectivity, individual history. One can be against "official" reality, against imposition, against the coercive normalizing analysis practiced in the name of the real, and still be for the idea of the two lists. After all, what psychoanalytic theory (as theory) is doing is making sure the truths of desire, subjectivity, individual history, find their way, in some authentic form, onto List A among all the other things that are real.

Reason Since Lacan

People who like the idea of Copernican revolutions may be pleased to see two of them, Freudian and structuralist, coming together, precisely superimposed, in Lacan. Structuralism may be defined as appreciation, and theoretical use, of linguistic, or language-like, systematicity.

The fundamental idea is that of *place in a structure* or (in another expression) *role in a system*. This derives, as is now generally recognized, from the work of the Swiss linguist Ferdinand de Saussure, whose lectures at the University of Geneva between 1906 and 1911 form the basis of the *Cours de linguistique générale* published in 1915 (1983). The linguistic sign, according to Saussure, is "une entité psychique à deux faces": "significant [signifier]," understood as an acoustic image; and "signifié [signified]," understood as a concept.[42] The two faces of the sign are inseparable, strictly correlative. On the traditional, pre-Saussurian view, the word *dog*, for example, was itself the sign understood as standing for or pointing to or representing or evoking—in a word, signifying—some independent thing. We understand the meaning of a sign—such as the word *dog*—if, and only if, we know what thing in the world or in ourselves it is linked to, much as we understand the meaning of a proper name if, and only if, we know whose name it is. For Saussure, a word, like *dog* is a sound with conceptual significance. This does not mean that words are sounds that signify, or represent, concepts. Unlike 'representation' and 'world' which belong to the old view, 'signifier' and 'signified' are strict correlatives, glued together with the strongest possible logical glue.

If the indissoluable unity, sound-with-conceptual-significance, does not achieve this status by being something like a representation, how does it come to be a sign? The answer (in schematic form) is: by being, and only by being, part of a language and having a use governed by a set of language-constitutive rules.

Saussure explains this by analogy with the game of chess. How does a piece of wood of a given shape become a knight? Its knighthood does not depend on, and so cannot be deduced from, its physical characteristics. The wood need not resemble knights or anything else. (This is Saussure's famous "l'arbtraire du signe [the arbitrary character of the sign].") The piece of wood is a knight because, and only because, it is recognized (in both the perceptual and legal senses) to play a certain role in the game. Its *value* depends on its differential place within a certain structure, the system of chess.[43]

It is one thing to summarize Saussure's basic ideas, another thing to try to say what happens to them in Lacan. Still I think we can say, as a rough generalization, that Lacan accepts, and sometimes even uses in fairly straightforward ways, many of the ideas of Saussure. Both see the individual as powerless against the mass of previously constituted, linguistically determined, meanings. Lacan would agree with Saussure that language is "le produit social déposé dans le cerveau de chacun (the social product deposited in everybody's head)."[44] As Anthony Wilden put it in his discussion of Lacan, "The symbolic order of language awaits the child at birth. . . ."[45] The language of one's parents, *their* categorization, is, to begin with and for a very long time thereafter, irresistible.

Perhaps the most often repeated "saying" of Lacan is that "l'inconscient est structuré comme un langage (the unconscious is structured like a language)."[46] This is, of course, a great deal easier to repeat than to understand. Here, I simply want to remark that this famous saying would not have much point unless we already understand that language is structured like a language, that is, like a linguistic system *à la* Saussure. Let us, for narrative simplicity, credit Saussure with the discovery of linguistic systematicity, with the idea that any "piece" within the system is defined differentially (or as an excluder) relative to all the other "pieces" that can be, or could have been, put into play in its stead. Various structuralisms then arise by applying systematicity to different domains. So Lévi-Strauss applies systematicity to kinship, Barthes to fashion.

This does not quite work for Lacan because the unconscious does not just speak something *like* French (or whatever the language of the analysandum); it seems to speak, to play with, to reveal itself in the interstices of, French itself. Its puns are French puns; its *Witz* French *Witz*, its silence French silence. This may connect with the Lacanian privileging of *signifiant* over *signifié*. In Saussure, we know *signifiant* was a psychic registration of a concrete sound that got its point, as a bit of language, through its arbitrary connection with a concept. Once conceptual significance is brought in, we can understand the relation and play of ideas, the figures and perversions of thought. It is much harder to conceive the process in terms of the "réseau des signifiants (network of signifiers)"[47] in isolation. Our difficulty doubtless reveals an unclarified bias in favor of the conceptual and correlative, forgetting that "langage qui est l'instrument de la parole, est quelque chose de matériel (language which is the instrument of speech is something material)."[48] Beneath abstract structures and conceptual meaning, there is "la modulation d'une voix humaine," "les mots déjà connus," "la voix du cher bien-aimé," "le côté coeur, la conviction agissante d'individu à individu."[49]

As suggested in the introductory section, it does not work with Lacan, anymore than with Wittgenstein, to try to assemble the main doctrines in a tidy system. One finds in reading Lacan enormous suggestivity, multiform virtuality. In the section "du reseau des signifiants," he pictures Freud addressing the subject: *"Ici, dans le champ du rêve, tu es chez toi."*[50] This is comfortable and genial and (despite his reputation for difficulty and a kind of intellectual fierceness) not uncharacteristic of Lacan. Finally, let me quote the sentence I was thinking of when I titled this essay: "Il y a des surprises en ces affaires de discours, c'est même là le fait de l'inconscient,"[51] which Hollier, Krauss, and Michelson translate, "There are surprises in these matters of discourse; that is, indeed, the point of the unconscious."[52]

Notes

1. René Girard, *Mensonge romantique et Vérité romanesque* (Paris: Grasset, 1961), 69-99.

2. Mary Douglas, *In the Active Voice* (London: Routledge and Kegan Paul, 1982), 292.

3. Jacques Lacan, *Ecrits I* (Paris: Editions du Seuil [Collection Points], 1966), 249.

4. Malcolm Bowie, *Freud, Proust, and Lacan: Theory as Fiction* (Cambridge: Cambridge University Press, 1987), 100.

5. Jacques Lacan, *Le Séminaire/livre I/Les écrits techniques de Freud* (Paris: Editions du Seuil, 1975), 8.

6. Ibid., 7-8.

7. Jean-Luc Nancy and Philip Lacoue-Labarthe, *Le titre de la lettre* (Paris: Editions Galilee, 1973), 43.

8. Lacan, *Ecrits*, 143.

9. Brice Benvenuto and Roger Kennedy, *The Works of Jacques Lacan: An Introduction* (New York: St. Martin's Press, 1986), 62.

10. Louis Althusser, *Positions* (Paris: Editions sociales, 1976), 39.

11. Benvenuto and Kennedy, *Works of Jacques Lacan*, 62.

12. Paul Veyne, *Les Grecs ont-ils cru à leurs mythes?* (Paris: Editions du Seuil, 1983), 11.

13. O. Mannoni, *Clefs pour l'Imaginaire ou l'Autre Scène* (Paris: Editions du Seuil, 1969), 9-35.

14. Serge Leclaire, *Psychanalyser* (Paris: Editions du Seuil, 1968), 14-15.

15. Jacques Lacan, *Le Séminaire/livre II, Le moi dans la théorie de Freud et dans la technique de la psychanalyse* (Paris: Editions du Seuil, 1978), 89.

16. William James Earle, "What Philosophers Talk About When They Talk About Sex," in *The Philosophical Forum* 16 (Spring, 1985): 157-79.

17. Amartya Sen, *Resources, Values, and Development* (Cambridge, Mass.: Harvard University Press, 1984), 452-53.

18. Lacan, *Ecrits*, 277.

19. Ibid., 115.

20. Ibid., 278.

21. J. Laplanche and J.-B. Pontalis, *Vocabulaire de la psychanalyse* (Paris: Presses Universitaires de France, 1967), 360.

22. Sigmund Freud, *Studienausgabe/Band V/Sexualleben* (Frankfurt-am-Main: Fischer Taschenbuch Verlag, 1982), 58.

23. Laplanche and Pontalis, *Vocabulaire de la Psychanalyse*, 203.

24. Michel Tournier, *Le vol du vampire. Notes de Lecture* (Paris: Mercure de France, 1981), 389.

25. Lacan, *Ecrits I*, 277.

26. Ibid., 288-89.

27. Jon Elster, *Sour Grapes. Studies in the Subversion of Rationality* (Cambridge: Cambridge University Press, 1983), 111.

28. Ibid., 138.

29. Tony Tanner, *Adultery in the Novel. Contract and Transgression* (Baltimore: Johns Hopkins University Press, 1979).

30. Freud, *Studienaussgabe*, 61.

31. Girard, *Mensonge romantique*, 111.

32. Lacan, *Ecrits I*, 286.

33. George Ainslie, "Beyond Microeconomics. Conflict Among Interests in a Multiple Self as a Determinant of Value," in *The Multiple Self*, ed. Jon Elster (Cambridge: Cambridge University Press, 1982), 156.

34. Girard, *Mensonge romantique*, 78.

35. Ibid., 105.

36. Ibid., 108.

37. Ibid., 104.

38. Lacan, *Ecrits*, 277.

39. Ibid., 68.

40. Lacan, *Le Séminaire/livre I*, 24.

41. Ibid.

42. Ferdinand de Saussure, *Cours de linguistique generale. Edition critique,* préparée par Tullio de Mauro (Paris: Payot, 1983), 99.

43. Ibid., 125-26 and 153-54.

44. Ibid., 44.

45. Anthony Wilden, *System and Structure. Essays in Communication* (New York: Barnes and Noble, 1972), 23-24.

46. Lacan, *Le Séminaire/livre XI/Les Quatre concepts fondamentaux de la psych-analyse* (Paris: Editions du Seuil, 1973), 23.

47. Ibid., 43-51.

48. Lacan, *Le Séminaire/livre II,* 105.

49. Ibid.

50. Lacan, *Le Séminaire/livre XI,* 45.

51. Lacan, *Télévision (Paris: Editions du Seuil, 1974), 27.*

52. *Lacan, "Television," trans. Hollier, Krauss, and Michelson, in October 40* (Spring, 1987): 18.

Works Cited

Ainslie, George. "Beyond Microeconomics. Conflict Among Interests in a Multiple Self as a Determinant of Value." In *The Multiple Self.* Ed. Jon Elster. Cambridge: Cambridge University Press, 1982.

Althusser, Louis. *Positions.* Paris: Editions Sociales, 1976.

Benvenuto, Bice and Roger Kennedy. *The Works of Jacques Lacan. An Introduction.* New York: St. Martin's Press, 1986.

Bowie, Malcolm. *Freud, Proust, and Lacan: Theory as Fiction.* Cambridge: Cambridge University Press, 1987.

Douglas, Mary. *In the Active Voice.* London: Routledge and Kegan Paul, 1982.

Earle, William James. "What Philosophers Talk About When They Talk About Sex." In *The Philosophical Forum* 16, no. 3 Spring, 1985: 157-79.

Elster, Jon. *Sour Grapes. Studies in the Subversion of Rationality.* Cambridge: Cambridge University Press, 1983.

――――. *The Multiple Self.* Cambridge: Cambridge University Press, 1986.

Freud, Sigmund. *Studienausgabe. Band V, Sexualleben.* Frankfurt―am-Main: Fischer Taschenbuch Verlag, 1982.

Girard, René. *Mensonge romantique et Vérité romanesque.* Paris: Grasset, 1961.

Lacan, Jacques. *Ecrits.* Paris: Editions du Seuil [Collection Points], 1966.

――――. *Le Séminaire. Livre XI, Les Quatre concepts fondamentaux de la psychanalyse.* Paris: Editions du Seuil, 1973.

――――. *Télévision.* Paris: Editions du Seuil, 1974.

――――. *Le Séminaire. Livre I, Les écrits techniques de Freud.* Paris: Editions du Seuil, 1975.

――――. *Le Séminaire. Livre II, Le moi dans la theorie de Freud et dans la technique de la psychanalyse.* Paris: Editions du Seuil, 1978.

――――. "Television." Trans. Hollier, Krauss, and Michelson. *October* 40 (Spring, 1987).

Leclaire, Serge. *Psychanalyser.* Paris: Editions du Seuil, 1968.

Laplanche, J. and J.-B. Pontalis. *Vocabulaire de la psychanalyse.* Paris: Presses Universitaires de France, 1967.

Mannoni. O. *Clefs pour l'Imaginaire ou l'Autre Scène.* Paris: Editions du Seuil, 1969.

Nancy, Jean-Luc and Philippe Lacoue-Labarthe. *Le titre de la lettre.* Paris: Editions Galilée, 1973.

Saussure, Ferdinand de. *Cours de linguistique generale. Edition critique.* Preparée par Tullio de Mauro. Paris: Payot, 1983.

Sen, Amartya. *Resources, Values, and Development.* Cambridge, Mass.: Harvard University Press, 1984.

Tanner, Tony. *Adultery in the Novel. Contract and Transgression.* Baltimore: Johns Hopkins University Press, 1979.

Tournier, Michel. *Le vol du vampire. Notes de Lecture.* Paris: Mercure de France, 1981.

Veyne, Paul. *Les Grecs ont-ils cru à leurs mythes?* Paris: Editions du Seuil, 1983.

Wilden, Anthony. *System and Structure. Essays in Communication.* New York: Barnes and Noble, 1972.

Summary

David Crownfield

The contributors to this volume are in general agreement that Lacan's work is subversive of basic Enlightenment assumptions about the subject, the world, and the nature of knowledge. William Earle draws attention, within this general consensus, to the undermining of the Enlightenment assumption that desires are, like needs, inherently describable and susceptible of satisfaction. Earle rightly notes that Lacan (and, indeed, Freud, whether he knew it or not) systematically contradicts this assumption, showing the inherent ambiguity and nonsatisfiability of desire. We have seen a similar point made in Carl Raschke's criticism of Frederick Jameson's Marxist response to Lacan; but Earle states it in a completely general form—indeed, I shall suggest, he does not always realize the full scope of his own generalization.

Earle also finds in Lacan a subversion of the Enlightenment's ideal of neutral and objective observation of the natural and salient features of the world, rightly noting that observation is naturally conditioned by language: not just, of course, the general forms of language but specific semantic prefigurations of observation. In addition, through his illustration of the victim of a New York street scam who is simultaneously aware of the objective facts that point to deception, and caught up in the fantasy of winning, he shows how the decentering of the subject so thematic in Lacan refuses the possibility of a unified objectivity.

At the same time, Earle talks of religion in terms of beliefs in payouts deferred to the hereafter, of faith as belief without evidence, generating an incommensurability between inside and outside, perhaps externally describable as a reaction formation against evidence, rationally defensible belief, and established knowledge. These terms, normally associated with Cartesian subjects and their external relations to the neutrally observable world, appear unaffected by the questions Lacan has raised about the possibility of such a subject and such a world. Indeed, Earle says the Freud-Lacan view of the psyche is preferable to that of the Enlightenment "because it is objectively more correct." It seems to me that the whole *philosophical* issue raised by the Freud-Lacan critique is precisely how rationality, intelligibility, and truth function after such ideas of "objectively correct" views of the psyche have proven illusory. Earle holds to a view of public, objective-cognitive advance, getting things more right than before, even about the psyche. This advance is indeed difficult, subject to inertia, instability, inner self-division, and other "impediments," but it is still the proper goal of rational inquiry. In contrast, consider Raschke's observation, above, that "subjectivity is not an object" in Lacan. Heidegger, as well as Lacan, would hold that such a model of truth and knowledge conceals its own temporal, historical, self-subverting features in an illusory quest for mastery of knowledge, of the world, of the Other.

An important section of Earle's paper is taken up with the analysis of desire. His contrast of desire and need is helpful (though his terminology, in acknowledging both "needlike" and "nonneedlike" desires, loses some of the sharpness of Lacan's dichotomy). His discussion of nonneedlike" desires, which correspond to what in Lacan is simply "desire", is quite illuminating. The paradigm of desire is sexuality. This cannot be reduced to biological instinct. (Freud, indeed, located *Trieb* on the interface of the biological and the psychological.) It is rather in large part a function of culturally specific myth and code. (He cites de Rougemont here; Foucault's history of sexuality, too, is precisely a study of such myths and codes that constitute sexuality in specific settings.)

Desire connives at its own insatisfaction; apparent objects of desire are treated as mere signs we pass by. "Desire is always desire for something else . . . a metonymy. A bird in hand is worth less than one in the bush. We subvert stable payout structures for the sake of something always else. Earle does not go on to make explicit, as Lacan does, that this is the very structure of desire: there is *nothing but* a pretext that this or that, or anything, could satisfy it. He does, however, go on to a discussion of "desire and hallucination," which deals in some detail with the distortive role of desire in perception and interpretation of others. But his suggestion that fantasy fails to satisfy desire because it suffers from "a shortage of scarcity" still perpetuates the illusion he thought he had dispelled, that desire is a sort of thing that *ought* to be susceptible of satisfaction. As I read Lacan, desire could not be satisfied by fantasy precisely because, for any x, desire can, *because of what desire is*, not be satisfied by x.

We may stop a moment here on Earle's image of television and desire. The medium, the screen, awards its populace a specious glamour, a kind of intimation of inaccessibility. Desire works, like television, as a presentational medium, giving its objects this specious glamour and concurrent inaccessibility. This is an interesting contrast with Vahanian's use of the image of the screen, where everything is present, explicit, as in language. The key difference, I think, is that for Vahanian language is a screen on which *all* is presented and played, while for Earle the screen is in contrast with a world on *this* side of the screen where reality is more directly available. Desire "televises" its objects; but Earle does not suppose that desire televises *all* objects. At the end of his discussion of Proust on this point, he says, "There is something special about *les Guermantes*, but it is literally, nominal, purely significant." What distinguishes Earle from Vahanian, and from Taylor, Winquist, and Raschke as well, I think, is that he does not consider this pure nominality to be the universal case.

What about religion? Is desire ultimately rooted, as for Augustine, in a hunger for the infinite, an appetite for the divine? The discussions of the Other in Wyschogrod's and Vahanian's essays seem to point toward an affirmative answer, though Lacan appears not to go that way. (The essay on "God and the Jouissance of [sic] Woman" associates God with the Other as real in *jouissance*. But *jouissance* seems to be in contrast to desire, as a connection with the real or the Other that desire subverts. While this might be given an Augustinian reading, I reserve judgment.) Earle draws attention to this question, but he does not take a position on it himself.

Earle then discusses the question of reason and religion since Freud as a question of adjudication of truth claims. I have already indicated that I think the Freud-Lacan critique of the Enlightenment makes that a dead issue. Specifically, I think that includes the notion that there can be (essentially universal and culture-free) lists of the real things and the unreal things. Of course we could make such lists, and would be saying something descriptive of our sense of reality and truth. But they are *our* lists, in relation to our others and our preorganized world. They are not the inventory of objects of a transcendental subject. This part of Earle's discussion, then, does not help me with the problem of Lacan and theological discourse.

Near the end of Earle's consideration of the relation of Lacan to Saussure, he raises a question that I think is quite germane to our general topic. He finds it (appropriately) difficult to understand the Lacanian privileging of the signifier over the signified. I want to try an answer that I think leads toward the heart of our topic. Saussure held that the sign (signifier/signified as a two-sided unity) divides, in its differences from other signs, both the domain of the signifying and the domain of the signifiable, in correlate ways: not a correspondence theory but a differentiating of the signifiable through phonemic differentiation of the signifiers. ("The linguistic fact can therefore be pictured in its totality—that is, language—as a series of contiguous subdivisions marked off on both the indefinite plane of jumbled ideas ... and on the equally vague plane of sounds.* For Lacan, the signifiers, through condensation and displacement, the metaphor and metonymy of the unconscious, differ in ways responsive to desire and not merely to "the world." The signified, as a differential unit in the signifiable, is thus marked out in a way responsive to the initiative of desire, an initiative still traceable in the signifiers as gap, dissonance, displacement, slip. The attempt to reduce the signifiers to arbitrary markers of the (implicitly preexistent) signifieds would suppress this initiative of desire, locate those divisions language marks in the world in "the real" rather than in the objectification of desire, to stray.

If this is correct, then a theological discourse that seeks to be governed by the preexistence of its signified will necessarily repress the agency of desire in its signifying actions and go astray. As Taylor's *Erring* reminds us, going astray may be the only way to go, but a theology that seeks to be unerring conceals its erring and its desire. Its God will necessarily be constituted as object of desire, but in a way better understood by Feuerbach and Freud than by its own self-understanding.

Deconstructing and demystifying such discourse, opening the interrogative, then becomes an appropriate theological agenda. But also the attempt to specify the difference between the Other and any petit other, as in Wyschogrod's reading of Anselm, and the interpretation of the discourse called Word of God as promising the reality of the utopian potential of language itself, find their place. It is thus precisely at the point where Earle finds difficulty—the priority of the signifier—that we can locate the displacement introduced by Lacan into theological discourse.

---

*Ferdinand de Saussure, *Course in General Linguistics*, trans. by Wade Baskin, (New York: Philosophical Library 1959), 112.

Extraduction

David Crownfield

Ambiguity is the duplicity of a signifier that can be determined in either of two senses, but that is unmarked as to which is proper. Ambivalence is the duplicity of a desire that is suspended between contrary valuations of an object. *Ambiguance* (a neologism) is the duplicity of a duplicity that is in unmarked suspension between ambiguity and ambivalence. This suspension itself, of course, unmarked and suspended between . . . , is thus itself an ambiguance.

In Lacan, the duplicity is a radical one, in that the subject of the suspended desire is itself split, dual, of a different identity as desiring and as rejecting its object. This split is itself ambiguant: is it a "real" duality (objectively true, in William Earle's sense), or is it an evasion of self of the sort Kierkegaard analyzed so thoroughly? I cannot tell, and/or I do not want to know.

The reader of Lacan is caught in the ambiguance of Lacan's style, Lacan's thought, Lacan's significance. If what he says is true, it is about me. I don't know if it is true of me, and I don't know if I want to know. The undoubted ambiguities of his text involve me in alternative interpretations of myself, about which I do not know if they are what Lacan means, or if they are true, or if I want them to be true, or if the one who asks and the one whose life they interpret are the same I. So far as I can tell, this comprehensive ambiguance is "precisely" what Lacan intended (though that attributes to him a nonambiguant intention to be ambiguant).

Beginning in the text of Lacan, and spreading elsewhere, a discourse plays itself across the surfaces and gaps of this ambiguance, obscure, enigmatic, evocative, involving us in an irreducible diversity of reading, of differing over Lacan. It is not, apparently, a theological discourse. But are there theological discourses? If so, what happens to them when they catch or are caught by (can we know which? or desire which?) the Lacanian discourse? A resolution of ambiguance? Or an intrication of theological discourse in the ambiguant play of psychoanalytic differences?

Does theological discourse articulate and evoke the possibility of a true self (Raschke), a radical wholeness of the human (Vahanian)? Or is the question of self irremediably fissured, wounded, decentered (Winquist, Taylor)? Does desire have its *telos* in the love of God (Wyschogrod; also Earle's question, but he doesn't answer it); or is desire — as I have read Lacan, especially in response to Winquist and Taylor, and as Earle's argument implies even more strongly than he has acknowledged — inherently unfulfillable, illusory, subversive of every *jouissance* and every openness to the Other? Is the Lacanian Other an appropriate context for talk of God (Wyschogrod, Vahanian)? Or an absolutist Identity, destructive of the possibility of dwelling (Scott)? Or is it only in unconstrained questioning, refusing the refusal of the bar, atheological erring, that a perhaps "post-theological" discourse (*a via negativa?*) is possible, as Winquist and Taylor aver?

Lacan's radical diagnosis of self as split, decentered, imaginary, unachievable is reminiscent of Kierkegaard's exploration (in *The Sickness Unto Death*) of the self that does not will to be a self, that wills not to be a self, or that despairingly wills to be a self. But how shall we read the relation between them? For Kierkegaard, the self can be itself when it is grounded in the power that posited it, dependent ultimately not on itself but on the grace of God that gives the self back to itself forgiven and healed. The complex decentering of self in Lacan, with its mirroring, its ego-pretensions, its unconscious desire, its simultaneous invention and loss of itself in language, all reflect, in Kierkegaardian diagnosis, despair, lack of faith, the refusal of the self to be itself. But Kierkegaard's assumptions, that the self *can* be itself, that it can receive itself from an Other in a way that is not a mirroring, an artificiality, an irretrievable loss of self but is a gift, a healing, a restoration of self-abdicated freedom — all this seems to be, for Lacan, desire, illusion, further self-alienation.

Theoretical analysis will not resolve this ambiguance. If Kierkegaard is right, decision must resolve it — specifically, the decision of faith in the God of Jesus Christ. If Lacan is right, psychoanalysis can enable us to bring the gap, the centerlessness of life, the incoherence of self, to speech, to become reconciled to the human lot, capable from time to time of *jouissance*, but without faith, without center, without self. Perhaps the best way to close the book and open the discussion on our theme, Jacques Lacan and theological discourse, is to indicate where each of our authors situates theological discourse within this problematic.

For Charles Winquist, the Lacanian analysis, like the deconstructive critique of Derrida as brought to theology by Mark Taylor, precludes the Kierkegaardian affirmation as well as more traditional forms of theology. A Kierkegaardian Absolute, like a Tillichian Ultimate Concern or Anselm's "That than which nothing greater can be thought," can only mark the radicality of theological questioning. Theological discourse does not contribute affirmative content, disclosure, that might reconfigure the Lacanian account, its radicality consists in its posing in unlimited form the problem of desire, joining Lacan in unmasking the inability of the objects of desire (including God) to satisfy, and joining Lacan also in refusing the identification of God with the Other of desire or with the Real.

Mark Taylor does not speak here, as he often has elsewhere, directly of Kierkegaard. But with respect to the present problematic, concerning the conjunction of Kierkegaardian and Lacanian diagnoses of the problem of self, he seems to me to present an ambiguous picture. On the one hand, his endorsement of Lacan's critique of Hegel's view of self and his stress on the centrality of desire seem to locate him squarely on Lacan's side of the contrast I have set up. On the other hand, his evocation of the depth of experience as desire, the quest of the Other as goddess, the proposal to refuse the refusal of the bar (refuse the repression of desire), seem to assume a desiring, questing, and refusing subject, somehow defining and centering itself in these activities, as though the deconstruction of the ethical and religious subject had cleared the ground for the reemergence of the aesthetic subject.

In a very Kierkegaardian style, this seems to be a subject that plays over surfaces, and that disperses itself over these surfaces in a decentered way while repetitively playing out its unpossessable desire. Such a subject exists, affirms itself, in its erring, in its marginality, in its refusal. But for Lacan, even such a subject-existence is illusion, alienation, concealment. And for Kierkegaard, such a subject exists in despairing flight from itself. I am not always sure I follow Taylor, but if I do, it is in suspension between Lacanian illusion and Kierkegaardian flight that I locate his notion of the subject of theological discourse.

The question is given a somewhat different focus in Raschke. In his emphasis on the introjective character of subjectivity the Kierkegaardian problematic appears to be dislocated. The subject is an artifice of language, adopted by the dark intentionality of desire as a strategy of subjecting itself to the other whose desire it desires. The overdetermination of conversation, simultaneously by discursive signification and by the semiotics of desire, provides its protostructure as myth. Magic is the attempt to reify and manipulate the intentionality of desire as a hidden signified of the discourse, suppressing its reality as desire. The Lacanian analysis then demystifies the secrets and disempowers the magical, by exposing desire as desire and self as its linguistic masquerade. The Kierkegaardian remedy is not available here, for the desire to be a self is rooted in the mirror image, in the gaze of Mother, in the dyadic absolutism that must be renounced to enter into the shared world of discourse. Unless ... Unless there might be, on the other side of the Law of the Father, in the very symbolic world of discourse, a *novum*, a healing word, a transformational possibility beyond the split of desire and symbolic self, offering wholeness in the language. This would be a theological discourse, indeed; but its description has taken us away from Raschke's essay on magic toward Vahanian's evocation of utopia. It is not clear whether Raschke would be willing to go in this way (though he does speak at one point of the "true self" beneath the Lacanian splits).

Charles Scott focuses not on the problematic of unity and disunity of the self, but on the question of whether human being must find identity in subjection to the Other as Law, or can dwell with others in a free play of sameness and differences. I have suggested that the Lacanian analysis represents not Lacan's program for human being, but a diagnosis of the structure of the pathology of existence, to be disempowered through acceptance of loss, disillusionment of desire, and consent to the rule of substitution and displacement. A Kierke-gaardian reading of the Scott version of Lacan would situate it in a despairing willing to be oneself over against the Father's Rule and the difference of the others, and in a despairing willing not to be oneself in subjecting oneself to the master Identity of the Other.

If what Kierkegaard means by faith ("By relating itself to its own self and by willing to be itself, the self is grounded transparently in the Power which constituted it."[1] It is possible, it would appear to be a requisite for the kind of benign human dwelling Scott invokes. Lacan's denial of the "own self" seems to preclude this possibility. But "Wo es war, soll Ich werden [where it was, I must come to be]." This saying of Freud's that Lacan embraces suggests something like Kierkegaard's "the self relating itself to its own self" — always remembering that "self" for Kierkegaard is a relation, or rather, "is not the relation but the relation that relates itself to its own self,"[2] which seems something like Freud's *soll ich werden*.

I suggested in discussing Scott's essay that psychoanalytic reconciliation to loss, the emptiness of desire, and the law of displacement and substitution might be prerequisite to being at peace in dwelling. Kierkegaard poses to this perspective the further question of whether such reconciliation is possible apart from the forgiveness of sins, from faith in the Other as God. Wyschogrod and Vahanian make further contributions to this problematic.

For Edith Wyschogrod, Anselm's fool represents the illusory ego, which think's it is the self and which says in its heart that there is no

God. The way beyond the illusory ego and its illusory desires is the recognition of God, the real Other, love of whom secures the existence of the self. The structure of this relation is compatible with that of Kierkegaard, but the dynamics of the analysis are very different. For Kierkegaard the relation is dependent on the revelation of the Other, and is accomplished as the act of faith. For Anselm, the relation is required by the nature of reason, by the very fact that we can conceive of "that than which nothing greater can be conceived." In Wyschogrod's reading of Anselm, the correlate necessity derives from the nature of language in its relation to the Other. Nothing within the domain of discourse is itself the Other; each signified is another signifier, displacing and deferring meaning (and desire). Yet discourse is founded in the gap between desire and the Other; it presupposes the Other beyond the objects of desire and the objects of signification. It is precisely the difference between the Other and any small other that requires the existence of the Other (not as an object, but as sheer Other; this is not incompatible with Winquist's reading of Anselm's God as a marker of unlimited interrogation).

What is not clear in Anselm and Wyschogrod is who is the nonfool who is the proper subject of the argument. Once we have entered into Lacanian ground (or groundlessness), the subject of the argument, the one who can conceive "that-than-which-nothing-greater-can-be-conceived," has disappeared. The mirror self is mirrored on a nondivine Mother; the subject of desire is a fantasy existence as object of Mother's desire; the linguistic subject speaks from a place that is nowhere locatable; and all this plays through the flesh like storms through the atmosphere. Each of these is other to the others: Mother is other to the fantasy, and to reality as well; language is other as Law of the Father, and always speaks of that which is other to language. How is it possible, and for whom is it possible, to conceive of that-than-which-nothing-greater-can-be-conceived? How is it possible to speak of the Other, when it is not clear who is speaking, or to what the Other is given as Other? Again, Lacan leaves this as a gap across which language plays.

Kierkegaard poses the possibility of the Other who comes as the forgiveness of sins, in choosing whom the divided self comes to itself; the emptiness of desire is transmuted by fulfilment. It is thus only "before God" (in Christ) that the true Other is disclosed, that it is possible to think "that than which nothing greater can be thought." This "before God" does not derive from the reason, from the Other posited in language as its other, from the analytic of desire and its incoherent subject. This is the point at which, for Kierkegaard, "subjectivity is untruth" (in the sense that faith is relation to what is other than the self, in the sense in which the truth is the appropriation of the absolute paradox, the "historical assertion . . . that the Deity, the Eternal, came into being at a definite moment in time as an individual man."[3]

At the end of all Kierkegaard's psychological and existential analyses, it is only the relation to God that constitutes the self as itself. In Wyschogrod's terms, the love of God precedes the capacity to understand the existence of "that-than-which-nothing-greater-can-be-conceived." The question, again, is whether it is possible for the Other to intervene in the domain of the symbolic in a way that can decisively reconfigure the situation. Can the Other become a petit other that transforms the impossibility of desire by preemptive fulfilment?

To make sense of Vahanian's essay, I must assume that he presupposes an affirmative answer to this question. The utopian power of language goes beyond our power to articulate any possibility we wish, bearing within it already the offer and promise of the grace that can make of the decentered self a whole person. The Kierkegaardian paradox is here given a "linguistic turn": the Other of the symbolic order can be signified, is signified, by a specific signifier, Christ, who does not simply defer meaning along the signifying chain, but kenotically ruptures the chain toward the Other as God — iconoclastically destroying our bondage to petit others and through the utter otherness of grace mirroring to us our promised identity as whole persons, in a wholeness that is not the alien objectification of the mirror or of the desire to be desired, but is the possibility within the symbolic order of loving and being loved, of changing and changing the world. But if this reading of Vahanian is right, why is his style so evasive of the specifics of Christian faith on which it depends? Is it simply that he wishes to avoid the risks of idolatrous petit-*a* objectifications, the use of his discourse as mask of the sacred rather than as screening of utopia? Or is there here a reflection of the same ambiguance that haunts our whole discussion?

It is difficult to make out how Earle would read the Lacan-Kierkegaard issue. On the one hand he notes the impossibility of the objective observer, the necessary insatisfaction and perceptual distortion of desire, the problematization of reason since Freud and especially since Lacan. In the context of these considerations the Kierkegaard-Lacan contrast can be opened up. But on the other hand, Earle holds to the Enlightenment goal of cognitive advance, to the realist notion of an inventory list of what there is that can be contrasted with a list of what there is not, to the problematic in which the question of reason and religion is the question of truth claims. To discuss religion or theological discourse in these terms would illustrate for Kierkegaard the sense in which "objectivity is untruth," as well as holding to a notion of a generic, self-coherent subject of knowledge, reason, and truth that, according to Lacan, is an illusion done with mirrors, as Winquist, Taylor, and Raschke all point out.

Yet Earle raises the critical question as to whether, behind and beyond its petit objects and insatisfactions, there is a teleology of desire toward God. Wyschogrod can be read to give an affirmative answer; Vahanian, though his treatment of God as Other is in important ways consistent with Wyschogrod, does not appear to agree. Indeed, when the issue is formulated in this way, I think Lacan and Kierkegaard have a common view, that desire is always illusory, and that desire for the infinite or desire for God is itself illusory — for Kierkegaard, a "religious-ness A" that is *founded* in the subject and not in relation to the Other. I find in Vahanian a position compatible with Kierkegaard and explicit in Karl Barth, that the intentionality of desire is empty, but the word of God preempts and transforms the empty and broken self-construction of its hearer, constituting in the mutuality of love of God in Christ a whole person without mirrors, fulfilled in spite of empty desire, granted the gift of dwelling. This fulfillment, this transformation, is for Vahanian always promise rather than accomplishment, horizon of possibilities rather than present possession. (He speaks of prolepsis, but guards his discourse anxiously against even proleptic present-tense affirmations.)

In this context, one might speak of Christianity in terms of truth claims, but the claim is not the subject's claim about which list God should inhabit in the inventory of the real and unreal, but rather God's claim that the dispersed, illusory, introjective, and artifactual subject may return from the far country to receive the celebratory welcome, and dwell in its truth.

This juxtaposition of the problematic of the self in Lacan and in Kierkegaard has perhaps served to focus some of the ways our authors regard the problem of theological discourse. It has, however, neglected an important dimension, which Scott has noted, but none of our authors has developed in any major way, which I consider to be essential to the topic. Discourse is interpersonal. Indeed, the decentering of the subject exposes the extent to which the subject of discourse is already interpersonal even apart from the question of the conversation partners. But, in addition, when we enter into the preexistent language, we do not enter simply into the whole Saussurean system, nor merely into the discourse of a specific familial microstructure. The words, phrases, patterns, images are already those that divide and unite specific communities of speakers. The Law of the Father is also the law that we must enter into specific contexts of history and community that have established the limits in response to which alone discourse can occur, and that thus we necessarily participate in the determination of the meanings and functions of what we may say.

Theological discourse already exists, is going on, has participated
in bringing us to our present practice of it. There is in Lacanian perspective no self-transcending existential subject that can take possession of theological discourse and originate it in a new way; there is only
a continuation of a conversation. I am concerned about the tendency
of some post-modern theological discourse to leave unsaid its partici-
pation in this discursive community, to celebrate a sort of solitary transgression and individual self-marginalization. It is in the real (shared)
world that faith occurs, and illusion.

It is in the world in which parents, professors, preachers, liturgical
texts, psalms, hymns, poems talk of God, of Christ, of salvation that
our speaking takes place. The individual character of psychoanalysis
gives a specific focus to Lacan's work that, contrary to the content of
his discourse, seems to some to invite a decontextualized deconstruction
of theological discourse. My juxtaposition of Lacan with Kierkegaard
(with his intense emphasis on the existing individual) has not sufficed
to bring this individualism into question. Thomas Altizer said some-
where about Mark Taylor's *Erring*, "At last we have a theology that is
completely independent of the church." If that is so, it seems to me to
represent a severe limitation of a highly creative work. The Law of the
Father, the preexistence of the other who already is in possession of
the language and who requires of us abandonment of the dyadic relation to the primal Other, is for theological discourse the preexistence
of the church, as a community whose significances are already lodged
in the language and make what we say accessible to a reader or hearer.

Scott appeals to our dwelling together, though not to specific theological or religious expressions of it. Wyschogrod takes as focus a traditional theological text, and reads it in conjunction with Lacan. Vahanian
practices a theological discourse always aware of the Lacanian issues,
but also always informed by a community of theological affirmation.
Winquist recognizes the extant theological tradition as a discourse whose
import lies in its images of unconditional interrogation. It would seem
possible for Raschke to go on to discuss the relation between magical
and theological discourse (perhaps in a way approaching Vahanian's?),
but he does not mark out that way. In Taylor and in Earle, I find no
overt engagement with the preexistence of theological discourse and
its community at all.

Our authors have presented a variety of perspectives on Lacan,
and on the themes of the subject, the language, desire, the Law of the
Father, the nature of the Other. They have in varying degrees and in
varying ways implicated theological discourse in the ambiguance of
the Lacanian problematic. Vis à vis Kierkegaard, they show divergent
perspectives on the question of whether the Other can unify the self in

faith or love. Vis à vis the extant discourse of the church, neglect or distrust seem to dominate, though not without exceptions. Only, I think, in the irreconcilable diversity of such approaches could the intransigent ex-centricity of Lacan's thought be engaged for this sort of reflection. Only in the conjunction of our misreadings can anything like a reading of Lacan's text occur. Only in a plurality of evaluations of the discourse of the church and of the Kierkegaardian issues of the coherence of self could the problematic of Lacan and theological discourse usefully be explored.

Notes

1. Søren Kierkegaard, *Sickness unto Death* (Garden City, N.J.: Doubleday and Co., 1954), 147, 262.

2. Ibid., 146.

3. Søren Kierkegaard, *Concluding Unscientific Postcript* (Princeton: Princeton University Press, 1941), 512.

Select Bibliography

Section I
Books by Jacques Lacan

Ecrits. Paris: Editions du Seuil, 1966. Trans. Alan Sheridan under the title *Ecrits: A Selection*. (New York: W.W. Norton), 1977.

Feminine Sexuality: Jacques Lacan and the Ecole Freudienne. Trans. Jacqueline Rose, ed. Juliet Mitchell and Jacqueline Rose. (New York: W.W. Norton), 1982.

The Four Fundamental Concepts of Psychoanalysis. Trans. Jacques-Alain Miller. London: Hogarth Press, 1977. (Translation of *Le Seminaire de Jacques Lacan, Livre XI, Les Quatre concepts fondamentaux de la psychoanalyse*.)

The Language of the Self: The Function of Language in Psychoanalysis. Trans. Anthony Wilden. (Baltimore: Johns Hopkins University Press, 1968.) (Translation of essays originally published as *Fonction et champ de la parole et du langage en psychanalyse, Volume 1* and in *Ecrits*.)

Section II
Books About Lacan

Benvenuto, Bice and Roger Kennedy. *The Works of Jacques Lacan: An Introduction*. London: Free Association Books, 1986.

Clement, Catherine. *The Lives and Legends of Jacques Lacan*. New York: Columbia University Press, 1983.

Davis, Robert Con, ed. *The Fictional Father: Lacanian Readings of the Text*. Amherst: University of Massachusetts Press, 1981.

_____. *Lacan and Narration: The Psychoanalytic Difference in Narrative Theory*. Baltimore: Johns Hopkins University Press, 1983.

Deleuze, Gilles and Felix Guatari. *Anti-Oedipus: Capitalism and Schizophrenia*. New York: Viking Press, 1977.

Derrida, Jacques. *The Post Card: From Socrates to Freud and Beyond*. Trans. Alan Bass. Chicago: University of Chicago Press, 1987.

Ey, Henry. *Consciousness: A Phenomenological Study of Being Conscious and Becoming Conscious*. Trans. John H. Flodstrom. Bloomington: Indiana University Press, 1978.

Felman, Shoshana. *Literature and Psychoanalysis: The Question of Reading Otherwise*. Baltimore: Johns Hopkins University Press, 1982.

_____. *Writing and Madness: Literature/Philosophy/Psychoanalysis*. Ithaca: Cornell University Press, 1985.

_____. *Jacques Lacan and the Adventure of Insight: Psychoanalysis in Contemporary Culture*. Cambridge: Harvard University Press, 1987.

Gallop, Jane. *Reading Lacan*. Ithaca: Cornell University Press, 1985.

Handwerk, Gary. *Irony and Ethics in Narrative: From Schlegel to Lacan*. New Haven: Yale University Press, 1986.

Hartman, Geoffrey, ed. *Psychoanalysis and the Question of the Text*. Baltimore: Johns Hopkins University Press, 1978.

Jameson, Frederick. *The Political Unconscious: Narrative as A Socially Symbolic Act*. Ithaca: Cornell University Press, 1981.

_____. *The Prisonhouse of Language: A Critical Account of Structuralism and Russion Formalism*. Princeton: Princeton University Press, 1972.

Johnson, Barbara. *THe Critical Difference: Essays in the Contemporary Rhetoric of Reading*. Baltimore: Johns Hopkins University Press, 1980.

Kristeva, Julia. *Desire in Language.* New York: Columbia University Press, 1980.

Kurzweil, Edith. *The Age of Structuralism.* New York: Columbia University Press, 1980.

Laplanche, Jean. *Life and Death in Psychoanalysis.* Baltimore: Johns Hopkins University Press, 1976.

———— and Pontalis, J. *The Language of Psycho-Analysis.* New York: W.W. Norton, 1973.

Leitch, Vincent. *Deconstructive Criticism: An Advanced Introduction.* New York: Columbia University Press, 1983.

Lemaire, A. *Jacques Lacan.* Trans. David Macey. London: Routledge and Kegan Paul, 1977.

MacCannell, Juliet Flower. *Figuring Lacan: Criticism and the Cultural Unconscious.* Lincoln: University of Nebraska Press, 1986.

Melville, Stephen W. *Philosophy Beside Itself: On Deconstruction and Modernism.* Minneapolis: University of Minnesota Press, 1986.

Mitchell, Juliet and Jacqueline Rose, eds. *Feminine Sexuality: Jacques Lacan and the Ecole Freudienne.* New York: W.W. Norton, 1982.

Muller, John and William Richardson. *Lacan and Language: A Reader's Guide to Ecrits.* New York: International Universities Press, 1982.

Ragland-Sullivan, Ellie. *Jacques Lacan and the Philosophy of Psychoanalysis.* Urbana: University of Illinois Press, 1986.

Ricoeur, Paul. *Freud and Philosophy: An Essay in Interpretation.* New Haven: Yale University Press, 1970.

————. *Hermeneutics and the Human Sciences.* Cambridge: Cambridge University Press, 1981.

Roland, Alan, ed. *Psychoanalysis, Creativity and Literature: A French-American Inquiry.* New York: Columbia University Press, 1978.

Roustaing, Francois. *Discipleship from Freud to Lacan.* Baltimore: Johns Hopkins University Press, 1982.

_____. *Psychoanalysis Never Lets Go*. Baltimore: Johns Hopkins University Press, 1983.

Schneiderman, Stuart, ed. *Returning to Freud: Clinical Psychoanalysis in the School of Lacan*. New Haven: Yale University Press, 1980.

Smith, Joseph, ed. *The Literary Freud: Mechanisms of Defense and the Poetic Will*. New Haven: Yale University Press, 1980.

_____ and William Kerigan, eds. *Interpreting Lacan*. New Haven: Yale University Press, 1983.

Thompson, M. Guy. *The Death of Desire: A Study in Psychoanalysis*. New York: New York University Press, 1985.

Wilden, Anthony. *System and Structure: Essays in Communication and Exchange*. London: Tavistock Publications, 1972.

Section III
Other Books Consulted

Chasseguet-Smirgel, Janine. *The Ego Ideal: A Psychoanalytic Essay On the Malady of the Ideal*. Trans. Paul Barrows. New York: W.W. Norton, 1984.

Derrida, Jacques. *Positions*. Trans. Alan Bass. Chicago: University of Chicago Press, 1981.

_____. *The Ear of the Other: Otobiography, Transference, Translation*. Trans. Peggy Kamuf. New York: Sehockin Books, 1985.

Descombes, Vincent. *Modern French Philosophy*. Trans. L. Scott-Fox and J.M. Harding. Cambridge: Cambridge University Press, 1980.

Gedo, John and Arnold Goldberg. *Models of the Mind: A Psychoanalytic Theory*. Chicago: University of Chicago Press, 1973.

Giner, Salvador. *Mass Society*. New York: Academic Press, 1976.

Grunbaum, Adolf. *The Foundations of Psychoanalysis: A Philosophical Critique*. Berkeley: University of California Press, 1984.

Hamilton, Edith. *Narcissus and Oedipus: The Children of Psychoanalysis*. London: Routledge and Kegan Paul, 1982.

Holland, Norman N. *The I*. New Haven: Yale University Press, 1985.

Homans, Peter. *Jung in Context: Modernity and the Making of a Psychology*. Chicago: University of Chicago Press, 1979.

Jay, Paul. *Being in the Text: Self-Representation from Wordsworth to Rolande Barthes*. Ithaca, N.Y.: Cornell University Press, 1984.

Kohut, Heinz. *How Does Analysis Cure?* Ed. Arnold Goldberg with the collaboration of Paul E. Stepansky. Chicago: University of Chicago Press, 1984.

Meisel, Perry, ed. *Freud: A Collection of Critical Essays*. Englewood Cliffs, N.J.: Prentice Hall, 1981.

Mitchell, W.J.T., ed. *On Narrative*. Chicago: University of Chicago Press, 1980.

Rieff, Phillip. *Freud: The Mind of the Moralist*. New York: Viking Press, 1959.

——. *The Triumph of the Therapeutic*. New York: Harper and Row, 1966.

Ricoeur, Paul. *The Conflict of Interpretations: Essays in Hermeneutics*. Evanston, Ill.: Northwestern University Press, 1974.

Schafer, Roy. *A New Language for Psychoanalysis*. New Haven: Yale University Press, 1976.

Sennett, Richard. *The Fall of the Public Man*. New York: Alfred A. Knopf, 1974.

Soper, Kate. *Humanism and Anti-Humanism*. La Salle: Open Court, 1986.

Notes on Contributors

DAVID CROWNFIELD, Professor of Religion and Philosophy at the University of Northern Iowa, writes in the areas of theology and the psychology of philosophy and religion.

DAVID H. FISHER, Assistant Professor of Religion at Santa Clara State University, has written on the relation of psychology to ethics and theories of narrative.

WILLIAM JAMES EARLE, Associate Professor of Philosophy at Baruch College of the City University of New York and a former Woodrow Wilson Fellow, has written the *Encyclopedia of Philosophy* article on William James and numerous articles on contemporary aesthetic and ethical issues.

CARL A. RASCHKE, Professor of Religious Studies and Director of the Institute for the Humanities at the University of Denver, has written *New Dimensions in Philosophical Theology, Theological Thinking and Religion, The Alchemy of the Word* and *Religion and the Human Image.*

CHARLES E. SCOTT, Professor of Philosophy at Vanderbilt University, has written *Boundaries in Mind* and *The Language of Difference.*

MARK C. TAYLOR, William R. Kenan Jr. Professor of Religion at Williams College has written *Erring: A Postmodern Atheology* and *Altarity.*

GABRIEL VAHANIAN, Professor of Theology and Ethics in the Protestant Theological Faculty at the Université des Sciences Humaines, Strasbourg, France, has written *The Death of God* and *God and Utopia.*

CHARLES E. WINQUIST, Professor of Religion at Syracuse University has written *Epiphanies of Darkness* and *The Transcendental Imagination* and *Practical Hermeneutics.*

EDITH WYSCHOGROD, Professor of Philosophy at Queens College of the City University of New York has written *Spirit in Ashes: Hegel, Heidegger and Man-Made Mass Death* and *Emmanuel Levinas: The Problem of Ethical Metaphysics.*

Index of Proper Names